smo400 3429
slo5
£12·99
792.028019 (Son)

DREAMWORK
for Actors

D1610614

Janet Sonenberg

A Theatre Arts Book

ROUTLEDGE
NEW YORK AND LONDON

A Theatre Arts Book

Published in 2003 by
Routledge
29 West 35th Street
New York, NY 10001
www.routledge-ny.com

Published in Great Britain by
Routledge
11 New Fetter Lane
London EC4P 4EE
www.routledge.co.uk

Routledge is an imprint of the Taylor & Francis Group.

Printed in the United States of America on acid-free paper.

10 9 8 7 6 5 4 3 2 1

Library of Congress Cataloging-in-Publication Data.

Sonenberg, Janet.
   Dreamwork for actors / Janet Sonenberg.
      p. cm.
Includes index.
   ISBN 0–87830–165–8 (hb : alk. paper) — ISBN 0–87830–166–6 (pb : alk. paper)
   1. Acting—Psychological aspects. I. Title.
      PN2058 .S66 2003
      792',028'019—dc21   2002152054

To Anna, Alice, Andrew,
Matthew, Jenny, and Elizabeth

Contents

ACKNOWLEDGMENTS

First, Rodney Brooks.

Robert Bosnak, whose work with me is the subject of this book. Much more of him in these pages.

Arthur Roberts, my friend and collaborator, without whom this book would not have been written nor would the theories throughout have been as imaginative. His ideas are everywhere!

Alan Brody, who told me, "Nothing is more boring than listening to someone else's dreams." Luckily, I didn't agree with him. Even holding that position, he managed to read this book throughout the process and offered advice at the speed of email. Michael Ouellette, who sacrificed his precious time to act with me. Peter Child and John Harbison, who encouraged me. Ellen Harris, who paid me an absurd compliment that I will never forget, although she probably has. John H. Lyons, Priscilla Cobb, and Mary Cabral who simply deserve to be thanked for a thousand things. Annika Pfluger, who created the diagrams. And Alan Lightman, who read a draft and told me to change only one thing. I listened.

viiiAcknowledgments

Monica Gomi, Charles Armesto, Fernando Paiz, Manish Goyal, Linda Tsang, and Tara Perry, who, along with Arthur Roberts, Robert Bosnak, and me, trail blazed this terrain.

Edward Kohler, Shelley Sonenberg, and Jen Tsuei, who confronted me with ugly truths, and then assured me that I could fix them.

William Germano, the editor of this book, a smart, kind, and genteel man, all qualities I admire.

Linda Tsang, Jennifer Tsuei, and Tara Perry, for inspiring me always.

And last, Rodney Brooks.

Introduction

Stanislavsky's techniques promise to bring the actor to the "threshold of the subconscious."[1] The depths of imagination lie there, beyond that portal. Stanislavsky's method (and the work of those who followed in his tradition, which includes me) assures actors of well-observed, truthful, and active performances en route to that font of unfettered "subconscious" acting. At the same time, it courts imagination and invites it to step through the door.

But what if we could explicitly contact the wild sea of imagination? What if we could forge links between the two worlds we know we

---

1. Stanislavsky referred to the unconscious as the "subconscious," as did French psychologist Theodule Ribot. Stanislavsky's initial psychological insights were derived from Ribot's writings (*Les maladies de la mémoire*, Paris Librairie Germer Balliére 1881, and *Essai sur l'imagination créatrice* Paris, F. Alcan, 1900) which affected him deeply when he was in France. Inner objects, affective memory, the notion of faith, and objectives were all drawn from psychological ideas articulated in these books as aspects of memory and creativity.

live in: the everyday world of assigned meaning and the twenty-four-hour world of potent symbols, tidal relationships, impulses, and chaos? What if we could harness the boundless creativity of our dreams in our waking life? What if we could dream the character's dream?

We are all familiar with three kinds of imagination at work. Allow me to present you with my own model, which I use to explain the work that follows. The world of imagination is comprised of the reflexive, the constructive, and the autonomous imaginations. Uninspired, indicated acting utilizes the reflexive imagination. It provides the rote gestures, intonations, actions, and activities known all too well by the actor and the audience. It has no truck with the unknown because it furnishes consciousness with the well-worn stories we all know by heart. Operative on its own, it is capable of delivering only the prepackaged, clichéd performance of shallowly observed behavior.

The constructive imagination makes use of an actor's connection to the text via his conscious observations, memories, thoughts, and feelings. The actor matches the pattern of his experiences against those of the character. He then brings his intelligence and talent to bear on the imaginary situation by constructing a personally enmeshed, re-envisioned universe. Stanislavsky's conscious approach to the unconscious maximizes output from the constructive imagination. Actors working in this way create satisfying, embodied responses. The more observant, intelligent, and intuitive an actor is, the more life he's experienced and articulated in his being, the richer these constructs can be. A good performance develops a linear relationship between behavior and underlying emotion. These actors convey why something is happening and act on the implied question, "What does that make me want to do?" This, in turn, creates a new why, which creates a new what, and a reciprocal relationship of action and reaction develops from the first moment of a play to the last, all underscored by truthful emotion.

Recently, I watched Anthony Hopkins teach a pair of young professional actors doing act I, scene 2 of *Julius Caesar*. They understood the ambitions at play in the scene, but Hopkins reminded the Cassius and Brutus that this was not the Forum in the eternal summer of Hollywood epics, but that (backing up from the Ides of March) the chilling winds of winter blew across the open square. Hopkins whispered, "Seig heil! Seig heil! Seig heil!" evoking the crowd's deafening support for Caesar, which resonated with the rise of another tyrant whose threat Hopkins knew from his own youthful experience. Hopkins stepped back to make associations between his own world and Brutus's that were rooted in the text, two crystal-clear examples of constructive imagination.

Most people create by making use of the constructive imagination. We contrast and compare, analyze the data, filter it back through our own experience, and often succeed in making something new. I do not mean to say that the unconscious has no part in that experience. Something meshes the data and the actor and allows impulses to flow from the new information. But we are *courting* inspiration by conscious application of indirect, volitional actions. When pure inspiration strikes we experience a jarring impact—contact with the autonomous imagination. We have dipped into that realm and emerge with something wholly new.

The autonomous imagination is distinguished by its nonvolitional nature: "You can't get there from here." It is independent and generative; something emerges that did not consciously exist before its appearance. Even if it contains bits and orts of our conscious life, it erupts into our world altering the equilibrium of energy, injecting something that feels radically new. Although it may resemble what consciously mixing and matching experience to the text might have constructed, it is more suggestive, eloquent, and momentous. It is often nonlinear and symbolic rather than literal. The contents of the autonomous imagination are whole and precise, recognizable though not necessarily immediately understandable. Their impeccable precision is so compelling, however, that our rational mind and all other imaginative faculties resign themselves immediately, or at least temporarily, to the force of a better idea.

Actors who transcend moment-to-moment reciprocity of action and reaction, who develop nonlinear associative dimensions in the relationship between emotion and behavior, often evoke autonomous imagination. (And it is these actors who have crossed the portal into Stanislavsky's "threshold of the subconscious.") We have all seen performances in which the actor and the audience find themselves in a territory they know fully but cannot explain. This great acting does not pacify; it is unsettling and demanding. In some fundamental way it refuses to answer conclusively the questions posed by the playwright. It *responds* instead. It is a present, living dialogue between the actor, the character, and the world. It does not ameliorate the anxiety of the audience (or the actor himself) but shows the choices they are making and disavowing at the same time. It goes further than cause and effect. The character reveals the sum total—at once—of his human desires and conflicts. He is an utterly human, expressive presence.

Great performances participate in all three kinds of imagination, for they are linked. If we think of imagination as the Earth, with the reflexive as the crust and the constructive as the mantle, then we can envision the autonomous as the core. Disruptions at tectonic plates, seismic activities, and releases of pressure from the core erupt magma to the surface and change the shape of the whole planet. In this way imagination is re-articulating itself, just as the Earth, in large measure, re-articulates its own geology. *Each manifestation is essential, each has its place, and all participate in the realization of a great performance.* So, while it is useful to think of imagination as having distinct levels, we cannot forget that they are part of an organic ecosystem—a world.

And the world they are a part of is our body-world. Imagination resides throughout the entirety of our bodies. Our work with actors proves out that an embodied, sensory response is directly linked to an outpouring of imagination, and imagination is directly linked to an outpouring of sensation. Where else could imagination come from if not our bodies? My partner in this experiment, Robert Bosnak, calls it "the dreaming genius," while humbly submitting that he does not know what that is. As for me? Perhaps imagination is inherent in everything. Perhaps it arises ex nihilo. But for the purposes of acting, it is more than useful to think of imagination as residing in a series of infinite regressions in every cell of our body.[2]

One cannot reject the reflexive imagination as inferior without doing damage to the autonomous imagination. And one cannot reach the autonomous imagination without traversing the reflexive and the constructive. The technique we developed using incubated dreams as a source touches on all three of these imaginative territories and gives each its due. It brings actors into proximity with the reflexive and the constructive imaginations en route to autonomous output, acknowledging them and using any richness that can be found there. The transactions among these three imaginative domains are like the tale of the Three Billy Goats Gruff. The troll under the bridge thinks he's entering into a clever negotiation with each Billy Goat.

"I am going to eat you up," roars the troll.

"Oh no! Do not eat me for I am the Littlest Billy Goat Gruff. Wait for my Medium sized brother, for he will be much more filling."

"All right. You may pass."

And over the bridge trots the Littlest Billy Goat Gruff. Of course, in the end, the third goat, the Big Billy Goat Gruff, kicks the troll into kingdom come, and all three brothers graze peacefully on the sweet

---

2. As an artist married to a scientist, whose dinner companions are often scientists, I shudder to think what they'll feel when they read that imagination resides in every cell of our body. But I defend my statement that it is useful to *think* it does for the purposes of acting.

grass on the other side of the bridge. Why didn't the Biggest Billy Goat Gruff just come and kick the troll out in the first place? Because that's not the way the story is told, and it's not the story imagination has told us in our investigations. All three Billy Goats are required to encompass the tale, just as all three imaginative phenomena are required. And who is the troll in this story about imagination? The ego, of course, another imaginative by-product, the one that has to be booted into kingdom come if we are to get to the good, sweet grass on the other side of the bridge. But the troll is never, never killed.

Our experimentation provided an ironic twist on Stanislavsky's caveat *against* counting on the manifestation of the autonomous imagination. We found it relatively easy to arrive there, but unless the actors were prepared with a strong inner structure, the contents of the autonomous imagination were so potent that they flooded the whole. The lesson is: There is no easy way out. As appealing as it seemed to create solely from the wildest source, the actors' bodies were not ready to accept the torrent of imagination. This technique that allows actors to disembark directly on imagination's shores requires a sturdy vessel. With that secured, the actor can enter the flow and let it manage her.

Dreamwork for Actors offers a new acting technique that intentionally generates dreams on a play. They are the characters' dreams created out of the actors' raw material. From these we establish an energized network that becomes the characters' body. This dreamworking is a technique that "evokes brimstone," one that embodies the "physical knowledge of images and a means of inducing trances," a technique that finds an analogy in a theater gesture to the gesture made by the lava in a volcanic explosion.[3] I will talk about the ecstatic qualities that the action of the dreams provokes on the actors and the

3. Antonin Artaud, *The Theater and Its Double*, trans. Mary Caroline Richards (New York: Grove, 1958), 80.

audience. I'll describe the steps we took, and our failures and successes en route to the development of a practicable technique. I will even analyze how and why it functions. But it finally remains as inexplicable as a dream.

CHAPTER ONE

Stories We Tell Ourselves

In some fundamental way, imagination's function is storytelling at its most majestic and minute levels. Or at least that's the story I tell myself.

We use imagination in life to explain life to ourselves. It arises in the form of regulatory structures, theorems, metaphors, and philosophies—all of them stories to help us picture the life we lead. The more lifelike the metaphor seems to a culture, the greater its currency. Thus, www.com captured the global imagination in the 1990s, as theater did in Renaissance England.

As a parent, and once a child, I experience the muscularity and sensitivity of storytelling. It is through these stories that our parents tell us our lives and provide imaginative constructs that enable us to succeed and fail. The obvious are the cautionary tale, or simply the word "boat."[1] Even before we are able to create verbal narratives, the

---

1. Psychologist Arthur Roberts reminds us that the first stories we are told are through the medium of touch. These sensate stories initiate us into the erotic and emotionally contacted. They provide the possibility of safety,

acquisition of language is storytelling. We learn that the object on the water has an abstract identity other than its concrete being, and thus we begin our inculcation in the realm of symbol and metaphor. We are able to translate from one realm, the thing itself, to another, the word-symbol for the thing. This is the beginning of our comprehension that life is comprised of levels of meaning and experience. By the time we get told imaginative cautionary stories that further organize our experience, we are past masters of the form and we cannot get enough of them.[2]

All of us, to one degree or another, require organizing metaphors to make order out of the chaos and disorder of our passions. These metaphors are leaps of imagination that set us apart from any other species as sharply as the use of tools. Octavio Paz, in *The Double Flame; Love and Eroticism*, writes, "Imagination turns sex into ceremony and rite, and language into rhythm and metaphor. . . . The poetic image is an embrace of opposite realities, and rhyme a copulation of sounds; poetry eroticizes language and the world, because the operation is erotic to begin with."[3] Meaningful sex is improbable without the converting action of imagination. Expressive language is impossible

---

love, and release from fear. An insufficiency or inappropriate kind of touching leads to emotional poverty, fear, and neuroses and, therefore, a very different imaginative construct about life and very inappropriate imaginings. It may explain a great deal about acting that these sensate stories precede verbal ones, for we have found that the coupling of physical sensation to words, experience, or memory is irradicable.

2. On a much deeper level, however, parents are helping children turn the wildness of sensation and emotion into words and metaphor, ripe for comprehension. Parents also may play imaginatively and tell stories that free children from the constraints of a world arriving fully imagined, and therefore static. The moment a child begins telling himself different imaginative stories than those shared by his parents is the moment of individuation.

3. Octavio Paz, *The Double Flame; Love and Eroticism*, trans. Helen Lane (New York: Harcourt Brace, 1996), 3.

without the converting action of imagination translating our desires and emotions. Meaning itself is not possible without imagination.

Of course, the kind of imaginative expressivity a theater audience is after depends on the collective story it desires to be told. In today's popular theater we crave magical realism. We believe that only a layer of truth is embedded in the conscious, "realistic" realm, and the Truth is found in the recondite unconscious. This reflects the psychoanalytic story many Westerners still tell themselves in the beginning of the twenty-first century, whereas Nietzsche, in *The Gay Science*, is clearly speaking about the audiences of his own time when he wrote the aphorism "Art and Nature."[4]

> In nature passion is so poor on words, so embarrassed and all but mute; or when it finds words, so confused and irrational and ashamed of itself. . . . We have developed a need that we cannot satisfy in reality: to hear people in the most difficult situations speak well and at length. . . . The Greeks went far, very far in this respect—alarmingly far. Just as they made the stage as narrow as possible and denied themselves of any effects by means of deep backgrounds . . . they also deprived passion itself of any deep background and dictated to it a law of beautiful speeches. Indeed they did everything to counteract the elementary effect of images that might arouse fear and pity—for they did not want fear and pity. . . . [T]he Athenians went to the theater in order to hear beautiful speeches.

The impulse to convert that which shames and confuses us into flights of sentient words is still part of the human experience. We want, we need, imaginative stories to make sense of the mute, irrational aspects of our nature.

---

4. Friedrich Nietzsche, *The Gay Science: With a Prelude in Rhymes and an Appendix of Songs*, trans. Walter Kaufmann (New York: Vintage, 1974), 134–135.

Imagination converts irrational social rules into acceptable stories. Here is one. When I was a child, Labor Day sharply set the
demarcation between white shoes and colorful clothes and winter
white and wool. This was a particularly shocking transition for Jewish
kids whose mothers bought them new suits of thick wool, often quite
lovely in my case, to wear to temple for the Jewish Holidays. Rosh
Hashanah came when it did, sometimes as early as the second week
in September when it was not autumn, but the height of summer's
heat and humidity. One year my mother bought me a fantastic wool
suit of black and white herringbone, a fashion-forward mini-skirt
and jacket and a vivid yellow wool long-sleeved turtleneck. It was fab-
ulous, but very, very hot. My brother and I donned our new clothes
with trepidation. Out the front door we went as a family, pausing for
the traditional family photograph. "The Jewish Holidays are early
this year," said *every* Jewish father to every Jewish mother. And *every*
Jewish mother responded, "It's unseasonably warm." Now, there was
nothing unseasonable about it. It was the apogee of summer, 90
degrees in the shade and climbing, 86 percent humidity—and it was
like this year in and year out. But the story our parents told each
other (and us) was that the Holidays snuck up on us like bandits,
robbing us of proper summer clothes. That was the terrific leap of
imagination that justified thick wool. "It's unseasonably warm." It
seemed to work for the parents. I cannot say the same for us kids.

Recently I read an article on annulments in the Catholic Church.
An annulment is the equivalent of saying, "This marriage did not
exist." Since marriage is seen as a contract with God, and a contract
with God *cannot* be broken, then to sever such a bond, it must be that
it (a real marriage) *never* existed, ergo an annulment. What imaginative story is more profound than pure denial: this event simply did
not happen. While it is difficult to comprehend the denial of daily
reality of a marriage, I finally understood what story the church told
its faithful and what imaginative leap it required. If this imaginative

story does not resonate with the listener, he or she will naturally struggle with the concept.

Imaginative stories are the sine qua non of our ability to understand the world, much less our shifting selves. The stories given to us by the autonomous imagination are invariably lifelike and precise, although often challenging. Michel de Montaigne tells a wonderful story about impermanence in his essay "Of Repentance." He writes, "I do not portray being: I portray passing . . . My history needs to be adapted to the moment . . . I may indeed contradict myself now and then; but truth, as Demades said, I do not contradict."[5] Shakespeare has Hamlet tell much the same story propelled by tragic circumstances, so the shocking story of impermanence must have been well and truly in the air the late sixteenth century. Did Montaigne's lively imaginative construct excite Shakespeare? It accounts for the blinding interaction among the past, present, and future. The present is just passing; observation itself alters the present and turns it into the future, and the interplay between man and his environment, or one another, changes us in every moment. Intelligent, observing people require a good imaginative story to cope with the slippery slopes of our ever-becoming selves.

Several years ago I was talking with a scientist friend of mine. He stated audaciously, "This thing you call rational thought doesn't exist. It's just a story about consciousness some people tell themselves. I never think." Although I wondered just who the "I" was who never thought, I was stunned. Now, I already knew my dirty little secret that I didn't think. I do something quite different than the commonly held model of discursive, linear thinking. But I had no idea that a scientist, capable of brilliant mathematical computations—in my estimation the hallmark of thinking—didn't think either.

---

5. Montaigne, *Selections from the Essays*, trans. Donald M. Frame (Illinois: AHM Publishing, 1973), 75.

It set me thinking, or whatever the equivalent is that I do. I realized that as a teacher of theater practice and as a director I do as follows: I read a playwright's text. She has already told herself a story so
she can tell me a story, the play. In order to understand the play, I tell
myself a series of stories. At that point, I tell stories to actors until
they can tell themselves a story that connects to the playwright's and
my own. They, in turn, tell the audience their stories that are constantly contacting the playwright's story, while at the same time the
audience is telling itself stories that connect to every story down the
line. What an amazing series of imaginative stories—when it works.

Of course there are other kinds of theaters telling quite different
stories. Polish director Tadeusz Kantor's theater militated against the
transferal of objects into metaphor. His actors' function was to be in
a state of anomie in order for the playwright's words to manifest
themselves. This is a story in itself!

An actor must tell an ageless story and fill it with newly envisioned
variations on a hoary old theme. It will be his story of the story. If he
is skilled and imaginative, these variations will delve beneath ornamen-
tation and open a world of insight into character and the landscape of
the play. Accomplishing this requires a good story to spring the imagination. A delightful story is one of imagination's greatest delicacies.
Imagination tells us stories, *and at the same time* there is nothing that acti-
vates and then nurtures imagination's presence better than a good story.

This two-way principle applies to all acting techniques. They
each have contained within them a narrative of some kind that catalyzes a fundamental difference in the way an actor experiences the
world. Imagination then does what it always does—it creates its own
story out of this newly generated experiential material. Imagination
volleys back a story that corresponds precisely to the implied narrative in the technique being explored. So for example, if the tale an
exercise tells is about contact between two people, the story imagination tells back to the actor is an interpersonal one.

The effectiveness of a technique is proportionate to how well the actor's imagination is captivated by its story. The better a technique is, the more it harnesses the themes human beings find endlessly interesting. However, a technique's fascination does not have to be immediately clear to be effective. Actual engagement in an exercise will lead to the creation of new information, which may reveal what the actor did not initially realize. He finds that he is comprised of more parts or more sensations than he ever suspected—that he is related to the world in ways previously unknown to him. This revelation will keep the actor focused for a protracted period of time, for it is a really good story with an unknown ending. And it simultaneously provides the actor with a productive haven during his time of not knowing.

The better an acting technique is, the clearer the actor's sense of *location*—where to go to get the good stuff—is. Inevitably this will be experienced physically. A good technique leads an actor to a solid sense that she will be able to find that place, that tangible boundary, and situate herself in relation to it so that information will unfold. The more physically conscious the process, the more reliable the results will be. The more conscious the actor is of sensing the boundary to be explored, the easier it is to get there. The boundary becomes an embodied place, not an abstract idea.[6] All good acting techniques

---

6. Fritz Perls and Paul Goodman wrote at length about the contact boundary—that border between organism and environment at which all experience occurs. They make clear that subjectivity (where most of us place the phenomena of imagination) occurs neither within the organism nor outside of it, but always—and necessarily— at the boundary between the two. This boundary is a constantly changing organ that registers the difference between each of its sides, and is the site, neither it nor me, where awareness arises. What we take to be a fixed, inactive wall is in fact an extremely active membrane, always engaging in a multitude of transactions. Given acute attention, these transitions and transformations can be sensed in every moment. The best theater techniques sensitize an actor to these newly drawn boundaries.

define the boundary that is to be attended, and then grant the actor a structure in the form of a story that enables her to approach and dwell there.

Consider the most abstract object exercise; let's say an actor is "breaking down" a chair. This particular exercise comes from Teresa Ralli, a member of the Peruvian theater company Yuyachkani. Let us assume that the exercise has only one given: break down the chair only in terms of your physical relationship to it in space. The surface purpose of such an exercise is to find the many, many ways the actor relates to the object and the object relates to the actor. So, the actor's body is an object relating to this chair object. After the actor sits on, leans on, and stands on the chair, and finally runs out of ways in which he commonly relates to it with his everyday, reflexive imagination, the exercise begins to take on new dynamics. At first he remains a body and the chair remains an object (although not necessarily a chair) as he finds new ways to put his body under, over, and around the chair, and the chair over, under, and around his body. Later, he further abstracts both himself and the chair, and they begin to create a unity, with differing tensions and fluidly created shapes. The longer he works with slow intensity, the more images and sensations arise unbidden. The observant actor will perceive relationships, either potential or realized, that issue forth as he works.

The shift in awareness and the expansion of imagination that the actor experiences can be attributed to two important things. The first is the freshly drawn boundary drawn around the body and the object. When the actor releases his rigidly held idea of both himself and other, and his limited sense of "chair" and "my body," a new imagining space opens that embraces them both. The dialogue between actor and chair never stops, and new fantasies and stories are told in that intersecting space. They are not the stories he would have told himself earlier in the exercise, but are now filled with a remarkable

autonomous images and memories filled with tenderness and passion. Attention to the boundaries must be paid! By simply redrawing
the field of perception great insights and newly discovered lands
emerge at these points of contact.

Equally, or perhaps more importantly, the actor has fully identified with his body. He accepts that he is "just" a body in relationship
to an object. He first gives up the shallow imaginative products of the
reflexive imagination, and as he moves with his body in an unpres-
sured way—there is no right or wrong—he discovers that consciousness suddenly resides throughout his body. His whole body becomes
an imaginative realm. The body invites the presence of imagination,
memory, and emotion, and continuing the exercise *as a body in space*
sustains these subjective entities.[7]

Contrast this object exercise of Uta Hagen's with Ralli's. Each
tells a story about the actor in relation to an object, but each draws a
distinctly different boundary between or around the actor and that
object. Here is Hagen's superb object exercise to be undertaken by the
actor playing Nina in *The Seagull*.[8] She wisely suggests removing the
character from the play's crisis and placing her

---

7. But, if the body engenders and then supports their presences at the party
then are they subjective? Are they solely the product of mind?
Understanding fully that these questions frame whole fields of research and
thought, that is, cognitive science, artificial intelligence, philosophy, and neu-
roscience, among others, I will only offer the evidence of theater's experimentation. The craft of acting develops strategies and techniques for actors
that seek to deconstruct the dualisms of mind and body, inner and outer,
observer and doer, in order to act. We focus on the practical necessities of
being alive in the moment onstage, and many techniques wholly succeed in
unifying the actor in these aims. I often wonder, however, what the subtle,
underlying significance of the actor's craft has to say to these other disci-
plines?

8. Uta Hagen, *Respect for Acting* (New York: Macmillan, 1973), 137.

in her bedroom, preparing herself for an outing at the lake; the life of
a landowner's daughter outside Moscow in the late 1800s. You must
look for, and identify with, and make use of not only your [Nina's]
clothing and underclothing, the details of your room (washbowls
with pitcher and soap and heavy linen towels, the kind of bed and
bedding, curtains, scrubbed flooring, icons, prayer habits), but also
with what you read, what's forbidden or allowed. How do you write?
By candlelight, kerosene, gaslight? If you write a note to Konstantin,
on what kind of paper, with what kind of pen and ink, etc.? Then
explore your specific task of getting ready for an outing.

Hagen's exercise places the boundary *between* the actor and object. She
then asks the actor to remain conscious of usage and *to observe* carefully her transactions with the object. The final two movements in the
exercise are identification—orienting the self with the object resulting in a close emotional association—and making use of all objects,
permitted and forbidden. It is a formidable exercise, and a benchmark
of the constructive approach. This detail is splendid, and an enormous challenge to any actor. Done thoroughly it will assure public
privacy by growing an actor's feet down into the soil of the period,
and into focused character behavior. When an observant actor rigor-
ously attends the boundary between her self and objects, it yields up
stories of Alençon lace delicacy. We do not often tell ourselves the
story of delicacy in these days (and Chekhov in performance has suffered as a consequence). This exercise bestows personal reference, his-
toricity, and their attendant behaviors to the performance.

The story the technique tells is to watch the transactions at the
boundary between self and object. The story imagination rebounds is
observational and behavioral; indeed a relationship can be brought
into existence between self and object. You must observe and then
identify with your observation, and finally use the object to fulfill the
task. The technique is not designed, in itself, to take the actor into

the domain of the autonomous imagination. Rather, in the line of Stanislavsky, the public privacy it creates prepares the way to the threshold of the unconscious. Ralli's exercise, on the other hand, places the actor and object in the same sphere and banishes the distinctions between them. A shift of consciousness takes place and the actor's attention is focused on the developing interactions. She is not observing behavior; she is experiencing the transactions. Working slowly and intensely and attending to the sensations and images that arise is part of the exercise. They are embodied, experienced, and allowed to pass, and the actor moves into another spatial relationship with the chair. This evolving experience permits the autonomous imagination to create stories that transcend the psychological and behavioral. Both are excellent object exercises, but each tells the actor a different story, and consequently the actor's imagination rebounds with a story that matches each exercise's essential narrative bid.

Taking nothing from the successes of many of Hagen's object exercises, her work on the area of "what time is it" always left me bereft as to how to deal with the deeper issues of time and the complex interactions that are time dependent. Hagen's work deals more with the boundary between the actor and historical time rather than the human sense of being in time, the victim or master of time. In the year 2003 we are, more than ever, at the mercy of ever increasing time pressures. The litany is all too familiar: The average beats per second of popular songs is a staggering 120 per minute, technology was supposed to free us but it simply freed us to work at home and work, and so on, and so on. How does one successfully break down her relationship to "what time is it?" Stella Adler and Charles Marowitz take two different approaches to exploring this boundary.

Adler describes an exercise in which she repeats the same basic activity but applies three different time constraints. The setting remains constant, but the times vary from lots of time, to nearly enough time, to not enough time. For example, you are expecting people at your home for dinner. The activity is setting the table. You set the table with an hour to spare and the dinner beautifully prepared in the kitchen; you set the table when you arrived home lateish and you are still cooking and the guests will be there in twenty minutes; and you set the table when you've just arrived home, it is too late to cook so you picked up take-out instead of preparing dinner lovingly as you'd intended, and you threw it in the oven to reheat because the guests will be there in five minutes. The technique tells the story of time creating a distinct set of embodied responses. The strength of this exercise is that it takes an actor and puts her in contact with something she understands all too well as part of the human condition—rushing. Time pressures cathect different body states, different body-worlds. Even if an actor can only indicate at first, her body will soon take over (to a greater or lesser degree) and the doing will create new information that stems from a new body-world. The different time frames reveal to us how relational imagination is. And once the imagination is engaged, it constellates a different body-world in any entirely relational way.

Charles Marowitz advanced the idea of acting respondent to the pressures of time—and to the creation of distinct body-worlds— several steps ahead in a wonderful and stressful technique that tells the story of time that many of us tell ourselves these days.[9] He developed the following exercise to give actors this sense of their bodies and inner lives in relation to time and pressure. It can be done by placing any character in a play in the center of the action, but let us assume that the protagonist is central to the action. A number of actors (A, B, C, D, E) surround the protagonist in a circle. "A" and

---

9. Toby Cole and Helen Krich Chinoy, eds., *Actors on Acting*, (New York: Crown, 1970), 431–432.

the protagonist (the protagonist and his mother) quickly work up the parameters for the scene they will improvise, followed by "B" and the protagonist (the protagonist and his sweetheart), and so on. Each actor goes into the improvisations aware of the objectives and the obstacles inherent in the play, but may find new ones as the improvised scenes unfold.

The director then calls "A" into action, and the mother plays the scene once through with her son. "B" is called in, and so on. When all scenes have had the opportunity to develop and conclude, the director begins calling the scenes in at random. He cuts them off at will (whether or not these are opportune moments for the protagonist or the other character) and calls in another scene. Soon, he calls in two at a time, letting them play their scenes simultaneously, and then removing one, but adding a second, perhaps a third. The protagonist must play all the scenes he is presented with as they arise.

Of course this is a virtual impossibility. When more than one scene is being played, one will not have the magnetic pull of another; and the weaker will be let slip momentarily. The actor whose scene has been let slip may find new ways to intensify his character's action because his need and intention are slighted. The protagonist has to attend to the neglected scene, but at the expense of more pressing, present concerns. Someone will be left frustrated. Someone's needs will not be met. Many people's needs will not be met. By the end of the exercise, the characters will be dragging on the protagonist for satisfaction and attention. One character may feel pity for the pressure the protagonist is under, thereby weakening (or strengthening) his or her case. The characters on the perimeter of the circle will resent or feel allied to others in the perimeter. Conversely, the protagonist will be fighting an uphill battle to meet needs, his own and perhaps theirs. The sometimes reductive quality of objectives is temporarily ameliorated; few people want solely one thing. Here is a technical corrective that allows this constellation of competing desires, so evident in life, to manifest onstage.[10]

Marowitz puts the actors (and characters) into a relationship with time that is so pressured that they feel like hostages of discontinuity. He is critical of the centuries-old tradition in which an actor "moves stolidly from point A to point B to point C, plod[ding] on in his old Aristotelian way, perpetuating the stock jargon of drama, and the completely arbitrary time system of the conventional theatre."[11] The boundary is continually shifting in this exercise, and that is precisely what conveys the embodied sense of discontinuity to the actors. At first "A" and the protagonist draw an interpersonal boundary between themselves that creates one body-world. Soon that boundary is wrenched away—arbitrarily—and "A" is forced to the perimeter. This creates a different body-world in which she is bounded by the whole circle. When "A" and "B" are both playing their scenes simultaneously with the protagonist, the boundary changes again and again. And every change is accompanied by its own body-world. The Old Aristotelian Way is disrupted—just as in life.

---

10. The actor intent upon achieving his objective in one scene at all costs will find himself stranded, as he should be, by the rivalry of contesting needs. Life is far too complex in this technique for the protagonist to take time with people behaving stupidly. Acceptable behavior within the realm of the character becomes defined. That actor who slugged the protagonist will instantly know if that activity fell within the realm of true character behavior because he can sense who did it: the thwarted actor or the actor-as-character. Behaviors that went unexplored in rehearsal because of limiting thoughts like, "My character wouldn't do that," suddenly manifest out of a need created by the universe. That punch may be dynamic and right, opening up a world of responses for the actor that he had disclaimed in his reflexive imagination.

11. Toby Cole and Helen Krich Chinoy, eds., *Actors on Acting*. (New York: Crown, 1970), 432.

Most plays imply the tidal pull of circumstances in time irrevocably changing the characters. And yet, we often see actors walk onto
the stage in a new scene largely innocent of the events and valences
that came before. By drawing and redrawing the boundary, thereby
increasing the competition of time pressure and warring needs,
Marowitz succeeds in evoking not only discrete body-worlds for each
actor in reference to another, but also the more complex sensibility of
the chaos of conflicting body-worlds, and the possibility of bringing
this onstage in the new moment. And that is exactly the story imagination dines on in this exercise. The time-pressured inferiority or
superiority of your embodied needs is a powerful inducement to
imagination.

Last, I'd like to take a look at a familiar technique that "bodies
forth" imagination in a different way, the Sanford Meisner repetition
exercise. In a stroke of simplicity Meisner relocated the actor's attention, moving it from internal objects, memories, and feelings (where
Strasberg would have it) and placed it on something dynamic and
volatile: the other living actor on the stage. By instructing actors to
put their attention on one another, Meisner's repetition exercises
operationalize the interpersonal boundary of individual body to
individual body, which is an enormously powerful arena of contact,
ripe with information, sensation, and stimuli.

The general rule of his repetition exercises is: Don't do anything
the other guy doesn't make you do. Here is an example of the simplest version of the exercise done by Meisner and Joseph, one of his
students. Each actor may only repeat what the other has said, changing the pronouns, until the other actor creates in him the need to
change the action (and therefore the text). We enter it in medias res.[12]

12. Sanford Meisner and Douglas Longwell, *Sanford Meisner on Acting* (New York:
Vintage, 1987) 41.

[Joseph] begins to draw again. A minute passes. Meisner, his curiosity aroused, stands up slowly and walks to the table where Joseph works.

"You're busy?" he asks casually.

"I'm busy."

"You're busy."

"I'm busy."

There is another pause. Meisner edges another step closer to Joseph.

"You're very busy," he says admiringly.

"I'm very busy," Joseph admits.

"Busy."

"Yeah, busy."

"Yeah."

"Yeah."

Again there is a moment of silence; then Meisner takes a step that brings him looming over the seated Joseph.

"I'm busy too," he announces.

"Are you?" says Joseph, hunching his shoulders over his drawing board.

"Yeah, I'm very busy," Meisner replies, leaning over Joseph's shoulder.

"You're very busy," Joseph says, and then in exasperation he stands up and says, "You know, you're preventing me from doing this!"

"That's what I'm busy at!" Meisner exclaims proudly.

It is not art. It is not playwriting. It is a training exercise, and an exemplary one. Exemplary because it asks the actors to acknowledge that the text they will perform when they act in a play is fictional, but the relationship they develop onstage is not. Each actor can and must affect the other. When they allow this to happen, each will inevitably re-mold the other's body-world—and *that* will be the primary text the audience "reads." But the distinction that makes this exercise so valuable is the attention to inner impulse it engenders in the participants. We humans have mastered most of our impulses to such a degree that we barely register them. The actor's job is to sensitize himself to impulse, so that he spontaneously acts and reacts in the moment, with interest, variation, and surprise (to himself, the other actor, and the audience). The boundary created by repetition exercises remains a vital and lively one through the actor's life because it is the font of responsive spontaneity.

The exercise supports the actor's imagination by providing a story, a context, that arises out of the present field. There is no prepared text, no event—nothing, except the other actor. The two actors place their full attention on each other and a field is created, inhabited by two people, which takes the pressure off the individual's need to supply emotions and substitutes it for a pressurized environment a deux. It's a lonely, scary world out there without someplace to hide while you say vapid things, like "I like your shirt," "You like my shirt." Denuded of everything but each other, the actors begin to sense the other in an interpersonal field. Their attention, now not on themselves but on the boundary between them, leaves the reflexive imagination behind, and impulse rushes into the breach. The quirk of an eyebrow, a sneer on the lips, or a tone of regard induces an impulse to action, and the repetition and action changes. Something happens—something is given in the environment—or it is not. A loving impulse can spring between actors who are engaged in a repetition about shirts. This boundary of interdependency becomes easier and easier to return to after the first moment an actor finds himself doing something genuinely prompted by the other actor. It exists between them, and is of them both. And once actors familiarize themselves with its location they find the authenticity, spontaneity, and excitability found in interpersonal contact.

Focused sensate engagement allows an actor to approach the boundary between herself and wider imagination. Maintaining this flow holds reflexive habits in check. Attention to the actuality of the present moment, whether it is in connection with objectives, the body, impulses between two actors, the relationship between the actor and the sounds of words, or any avenue of technique, invites the possibilities of new thoughts, behavior, images and feelings to emerge and develop. It is as if these potentials were there all along, but we didn't know where to look. This new material emerges only with disciplined attention to her senses in contact with the wider, or subtler, world. Nature abhors a vacuum and fresh material rushes in to take the place of old, and is immediately appropriated. The actor becomes identified with these and she lends them to the character. And even more importantly, the actor identifies the process of locating this informative boundary and can return there at will.

We think of the autonomous imagination as a wild seething ocean. But in point of fact it is not only deviant, impulsive, and crude, but also harmonious, calculating, and smooth. It is as witty as it is ribald, as deadly as it is playful. It is all these things and more; it is our humanity at its most revolutionary. Let's assume that we exist within the universe of imagination. No, let's go further and assume we are ultimately *of* imagination. Let us take this assumption even further, that our intangible thoughts, our dreams, our bodies, and everything around us—clouds, food, water, stone—are the active play of imagination. "We are such stuff as dreams are made on," and we dwell in a landscape of material imagination. By widening the field to the vastness of the universe the points of imaginative contact are boundless.

In the work I am about to describe in the next chapters, the participants will all behave *as if* the universe, including oneself, were living imagination. It led us to a remarkably fresh perspective, and sprang forth wildly imaginative acting.

CHAPTER TWO

Next Year Let's Work on Your Imagination

I had a casual conversation between classes with Tara Perry, one of the most talented students I have ever taught. I spotted her in the hall and—without really thinking about it—blurted out, "Next year let's work on your imagination."

Her work was already more fully imagined than most actors. She pursued objectives with committed, sensitive physical action; her expressive body and voice gave movement and music to desire and obstacle; her work was spontaneous and interpersonal; she personalized or particularized like a seasoned professional; she broke down props, costumes, and words creatively; her research was perfect. To add to this long list of talents, her acting was informed by a point of view; she spoke from a gorgeous self-reliant and melancholy inner voice that whispered, "From dust we come, to dust we go. Now, what are we to do with this moment?" This young actor didn't have an acting problem; she had acting strengths. But her comparatively little life experience limited her prodigious native talents. Would I simply have to wait until she turned thirty? Would a hectic life filled with experi-ence yield the *kind* of imaginative acting I envisioned?

What was I after? I sought the surprising. I wanted to be ambushed by what was utterly simple and true— not by flamboyant dramatics. I wanted to enlist the imagination in the service of those idiosyncratic things we see people do in life but rarely onstage. I wanted to watch a character's body betray her will and to see the sub-tly textured interplay of conflicting and simultaneous desire. I wanted to see characters driven by a rich, complex, and profound inner life. In sum, I wanted to see behavior that was so immediately recognizable—*but not immediately understandable*—that it would shake me to the core.

But how to work directly *on* imagination? All acting techniques are a dialogue with imagination, but they all, to the best of my knowledge, use something else as the conduit. So, for example, Nora Dunfee used phonemes of words as the trap to spring imagination, Meisner used "the other" and the interpersonal boundary, and Stanislavsky gave us the peerless objective to invite imagination to the party. Could one work directly *on* imagination with a consciously applied technique? Could I find Tara a bridge to autonomous imagi-nation that would transcend experience?

That night I had a dream:

I unroll a living map of the Great Northwest. Pods of whales and schools of dolphin feed in the choppy waters of the Baleen Sea. White caps surge and fall as I scan the map for directions. . . .

. . . I journey across the Baleen Sea to stop at Trader Jack's en route to the Great Northwest. There I find the sweets I promised my daughter, but they are corrupted by the presence of rats. . . .

. . . Arriving at the Great Northwest a play called *The Monkey Puzzle Room* is in progress. It is a site-specific event taking place in the narrow confines of a ship's cabin. Serious, proud actors don't seem to be doing much of anything, but doing it with great dignity, and I wonder, "Where's the action?"

When I awoke I thought, "How imaginative. How imaginative."

The following day psychotherapist Arthur Roberts and I met and I wondered with him, as one does with close friends, "How can dreams be used by actors?" They are the site of our most profound imaginings; could they be useful as source material for actors? Could actors willfully generate dreams on a play, perhaps on its themes, perhaps on scenes or conflicts or characters? Since autonomous imagination expresses itself most luxuriously in dreams, could a link be forged between the actor (and her imagination) and the play (and the playwright's imagination)? What about a link between the actor's imagination and the character's imagination? We envisioned an acting technique that gave direct access to this rich sea of imagination that envelops both actor and play and holds them in a common sphere. What if the actor could debark directly on imagination's shores?

Our thoughts naturally led us to Jung, who said,

Where must we lead our patient to give him at least the glimmer of a notion of something other than his everyday world, which he knows too well? We must lead him, by long detours, to a dark and absurdly unimpressive, totally unimportant and worthless place in his soul, by a long-disused path to an illusion which has long been recognized as such, of which the whole world knows that it is nothing. . . . [T]he place is the dream, that fleeting, grotesque thing of the night.[1]

---

1. Carl Jung, *Psychological Reflections; A New Anthology of His Writings*, 2d ed., ed. Jolande Jacobi (Princeton, NJ: Princeton University Press, 1970), 67–68.

Jung wrote those words in 1934; six decades later we postulated that by making use of the dream, we might be able to bring the actor— by long detours— to a place where his everyday life would hold little sway, and where he would be privy to realms of experience that were entirely outside the purview of his work-a-day waking consciousness.

A Pharaoh's Granary of dreams is available to us. But how to use them? Jung's process for "treating" dreams seemed the place to begin, and the notable Jungian analyst Robert Bosnak was the person to call. Synchronicity— that Jungian term par excellence— was at play here. Two years earlier, Alan Arkin suggested that I contact a woman who worked with dream material. She, in turn, had suggested calling Robert Bosnak as the leader in this field. As I was busy with other projects I let the lead fall away. But here was his name again at the moment I was actively tracking the scent of a new, creative idea. When the universe conspires, I pick up the phone and dial.

Robert was interested. We agreed that I should experience first-hand his process of treating dreams in order to place my intuition about acting within some kind of framework. For several weeks I brought dreams to him and he walked with me through their landscapes.

Jung understood that the dreamer normally experiences the dream as a real event. The map, the monster, or the Monkey Puzzle Room are palpable and genuine as they reveal themselves in our dream, and they take place in a vivid landscape. But when we awake and recall the dream—and especially when we recount it— we are distanced from its immediacy and tangibility.[2] The spoken dream

---

2. A complex psychological process (originally documented by Freud) occurs during the translation of the dream from experienced event to rehashed narrative.

describes a linear story because we translate what is essentially symbolic analogy into a digital language in order to communicate it. We focus on a detail and then move to the next in order to make sense of the total content. Dream content, however, is more like a sculpture than a film. In a dream the whole is given all at once and is encoded in the image.

Robert trained as a Jungian analyst, but like any creative person he developed his own techniques stemming from the original source. The object of his dreamwork is to re-experience the dream in its landscape in waking life, allowing the images to become re-infused with their original sculptural qualities. While re-experiencing them, the images are felt to be abundantly fed by personally significant symbolism. The idea of re-experiencing dreams instead of merely telling them would become a cornerstone of our dreamwork acting process.

During my early meetings with Robert, I would tell a dream straight through in anecdotal fashion. Then, guided by him, I re-entered the dream at a relaxed, unthreatening instance—never at a moment of crisis or intensity. From this starting point, Robert broadened the scope of the dream images by asking me how I experienced them in my body. Where did I feel sensation that simultaneously arose with the image? What was the quality of that feeling? I might not have noticed this sensate data on my own, but when directed to do so, it readily revealed itself if it were there.

To give an example from our first session, here is a précis of a detailed dream. Everyone in the world is boarding trains bound for heaven. Disgruntled angels conduct dazed and disbelieving people into the cars. In the next fragment I go to a rather dirty beach to swim in the ocean where many people are swimming. I am in the ocean holding a book and feeling good because I know the author. It was a complex dream comprised of several scenes, so Robert began the work at this relatively calm dream fragment. Robert puts me into the landscape with:

You say that the beach has dirty sand and a lot of people. What kind
of day is it?

Too cold for swimming but everyone is in. It is spring.

In my recall and initial telling of the dream I did not possess this
information. It emerged upon questioning only when I re-entered the
dream landscape.

It's cold on your skin?

I'm conscious of the fact that it is cold, but I don't experience that
physically.

Are your feet bare?

Yes.

And you're carrying this important book?

I nod in agreement.

Can you describe it to me?

Yes, it is an over sized book—the size of a coffee table book.

Can you feel its importance in your body?

Yes, in my arms and chest it's—No, it is not that the books is important, it's that the book makes me feel important. That's what I feel in
my arms. The book itself is filled with meaningless information.

Meaningless?

Meaningless. Shallow. It is glossy enough for people to want to own
it, but how many of them actually read it?

What's the feeling in your body of the gloss?

It pushes on my spine. I also have a carbonated feeling that tells me I'm excited. I'm excited by the gloss of the book.

Can you feel yourself into the gloss?

Yes.

What is it like if life is gloss?

Like I have reached the point of least resistance—like a diver poised in the perfect position to make the least splash when she hits the water. It is so smooth, like glass. It makes me want to just slide in—it feels like it's driving me to do just that. But there is opposition.

Where do you feel this opposition?

In my skin. It feels heavier, more mundane.

What is it like to have this skin that opposes?

It feels very, very real.

By fusing the dream image with my physical experience, its sensate and emotional content blossomed, suffusing my body. I was both the dreamer and the dreamed— able to observe and experience simultaneously.

Entering into the body or inner being of any of a dream's images—whether an object or a person—and experiencing it framed another key concept in our work together. We call this transiting. I could, for example, enter into the land on which my dream-self stood and speak from its experience of itself in the dream. When Robert asked me to transit into a character— a straightforward hypnotic suggestion made to me in my focused state— I could actively experience that character's reactions and feelings. Here is a brief example from dreamwork in which I transited into a polar bear in a photograph.

Robert begins:

So does the mother polar bear have the cub on her belly?

On her back. . . in crystal clear turquoise blue water, much too warm for polar bears.

Sounds like Caribbean.

Yes, and the mother polar bear is—you know when dogs are really happy and their fur is all plastered back on their face if they've been running, and their tongues are hanging out at the side and their eyes are so bright—?

What do you see through her bright eyes?

I look over my shoulder as I swim and I'm so happy. But my child isn't having the same experience as I am. The child experiences sheer pleasure, but I'm having the double experience of this pleasure and revisiting the pleasure of my own childhood. I'm giving my child and myself this gift.

After years of practicing the technique I remain astonished by the noncritical ease with which people immediately accept the penetration of self and other. Imagination adores the invitation to see through the polar bear mother's eyes. She was, after all, created by imagination and is of imagination. The genetic match is perfection itself. Whether there is delight or horror to be found in the image, imagination rushes willingly to the forefront and lubricates the way.

One final movement that ultimately found its place in our acting technique is bound active imagination. If asked how dream character responded, even when I didn't witness that response in the dream, I spontaneously imagined her response. Robert and I call it *bound* active imagination because it is bound by the data of the image. In our work we do not let the subject imagine away from the landscape and its contents. Although bound active imagination seems to denote that I willfully made something up, the actual result seemed far different.

For example, with regard to a female character in the first dream I described, Robert asked me:

And what does she feel about you?

I look at her as she walks away from me. She's carrying beach equipment up from the ocean. As I concentrate on her retreating back, the woman turns toward me—something she did not do in my recall of the dream.

> She smiles at me. Even though I am being impossible, she loves me unequivocally.

As I re-experienced the dream and inhabited its territory it became a concrete landscape that allowed me to experience its inherent intelligence. The fusion of the image with bodily sensation—and the attendant emotion—began to reveal the dream imagery as a mysterious, vital, unified whole that expressed itself in and through me.

Robert and I intentionally refrained from analyzing the dreams. Healing was not our goal. We didn't want to unravel the mystery of the dream's imagery. We wanted the images to retain their symbolic potential and to become grounded in the actor's body. Their meaning would come forth—as it always will, one way or another—but it would come forth later, in the context of, and in the service of, performance. We began tailoring the process more and more toward the embodiment of landscapes, evading analytical clarity as we could.

During these weeks I worked alone with Robert, the connections I made between the dreamwork and acting were exciting but tentative. I remained wary. Not only did I not know exactly what I was doing, but also the nervousness of entering terra incognita possessed me. To lessen my fears I took the first small steps toward applying the technical aspects of Robert's process to my normal work as an acting teacher. I decided to use the technique on a literal memory instead of a dream to see if I could turn it into a concrete, sensate reality.

I have a crisis of faith regarding the technique of affective memory. No teacher ever instructed me well in it, and the doubt surrounding my experience poisoned my desire to employ it. I know some are skilled at it, for example, my friend and colleague Michael Ouellette. He manages to create linkages between the physical sensation embodied in the memory and those the actor feels when she retrieves it. I see his successes in actor after actor. They do it well and use it appropriately.[3] The memory becomes an affective environment, not a hot bullet of emotion. But for me the technique remains vexed.

If we look at the technique as described by Bobby Lewis we can see the flaws that make affective memory a problematic technique for some, or at least for me.[4] Lewis begins: "The first thing to achieve in performing an Emotional Memory exercise is complete physical relaxation." The problems begin! My mind bridles at this impossible directive to relax completely. Confronted with the impossible, I have failed during step one.[5]

---

3. When done badly, evoked memory is only the machine that produces the magic bullet of emotion. This hot emotional state is then overlaid on a scene, and its effect often feels like a blunt instrument that gives muscle to a moment, and then hammers away on what should be nuanced, imaginative, emotional, and in a state of ongoing transition. Emotion is not the end-all and be-all of acting. At the very least it must always be in the service of forward-moving action.

4. Toby Cole and Helen Krich Chinoy, eds., *Actors on Acting* (New York: Crown, 1970), 431–432, 630–634.

5. Merleau-Ponty tells us that the "body is our general medium for having a world," and so to consider its rhythms as opposition to be conquered results in a misguided attempt that—if successful—must end in the cessation of experience! It would literally result in the annihilation of our world.

Lewis goes on to write, "Now start to concentrate on an incident chosen from your life that you feel will summon up an emotion similar to what is required in the scene. [. . .] Be careful you do not try to remember how you felt at the time." This statement is a distraction technique, and a good one: The conscious mind does what it's told while the unconscious is busy being oppositional. The equivalent of saying, "Try not to think of the pink elephants," Lewis's directive can be understood as: Remember how you felt at the time.

The following augments the distraction technique:

Rather, recall and re-create all the physical circumstances of the occasion. Remember all the details of the place where the event occurred, the time of day, how everything looked, who was there and how they appeared. The ability to recall and, more importantly, to re-experience the sensory impressions of the incident is of primary concern.

Yes, yes, yes! I'd be delighted to do all of that, but how? The color and expression of my great-grandmother's eyes are surely anchored to physical sensation in my body, but how do I go about working patiently at attending to the boundary between my body and my memory? If her eyes precipitate emotion, and they do, how do I tangibly fuse the image and the memory so it does not pass ephemerally into nothingness? The body is the file for memory, and it is through its experience that images arise. Working in the opposite direction, if I chose a memory to explore, it is only by patient, careful attention to the body as the memory unfolds that it becomes available as a source. How do I go about this?

Lewis concludes: "Now, in detail, go over in your mind exactly what transpired. If it is a properly chosen strong situation from your life, you should soon start to experience emotion resulting from the recall. You can then use this emotion as you step into the scene you are to play." I'll resist comment on the fallibility of the actor but not the technique. In sum, I find the story inherent in Lewis's description of affective mem-

ory unreliable. It does not engage my imagination seamlessly. It is full of
tricks and double binds that make me bridle. No wonder I cannot use
it. Its most egregious flaw—for me—is that it places the mind at the
center of imagination without reliable access to the sea of imagination
our bodies inhabit. Would I finally be able to make memory affective,
the source of embodied experience, if I put the actor's whole body in a
landscape charged with meaning and sensation? Here is the first experiment I did using some of the techniques Robert employed with dreams.

Linda Tsang is talented, purposeful actor. She works in an intimate, emotionally available way. Once she finds the emotional context for a scene she remains softened to it. She has sensitivity and sus-
ceptibility cloaked in steel—Linda is strong and smart. We trust each
other and have collaborated many times, and we always expect that
our work together will be beautiful. She was working on Helena's
confession of her love for Bertrand.[6] The confession is made to
Bertrand's mother, the Countess, Helena's guardian, only friend, and
her parent in spirit. The stakes are high; Helena stands to lose everything should the Countess take umbrage.

Five lines into the monologue and Linda was making only a gen-
eralized connection to the words and situation. After this mealy
beginning her acting gained authority. I stopped her and we talked
about the first line:

> Then I confess
> Here on my knee, before high heaven and you,
> That before you, and next unto high heaven,
> I love your son.

Linda understood the hopelessness of the confession: Helena is
not Bertrand's social or financial equal. Bertrand doesn't even think of

---

6. *All's Well That Ends Well*, act I, scene 3.

her, much less love her. But Linda had only an intellectual grasp of the precipice Helena stands on when she confesses. The act of confessing was not specific for her; what is at risk?

I asked her to locate in her memory an event during which she felt compelled to make an unpremeditated confession. I felt that a confession that burst forth would have concomitant physical reactions, and these were precisely what I was seeking.[7] Linda located a memory, and I told her that I wanted to walk through its landscape with her. She told me that she felt that her boyfriend, Dan, didn't respect the way she expressed herself. She experienced his correction of her syntax and grammar as derogatory, diminishing her worth in both his eyes and her own. After this introduction, she told the memory once through. On a particular evening they were to go to the theater together. When he arrived at her apartment he said several things that made her feel belittled. Suddenly, Linda's accusation that he didn't respect her burst forth, along with her confession of humiliation. She experienced the very real risk that this outburst might spell the end of their relationship. They fought for two hours instead of going out to the theater.

Linda and I began to treat this memory as an embodied landscape with an emphasis on present sensate experience. She sat in a chair and I asked her to tell me what she saw when she placed herself an hour before Dan's arrival:

I'm alone in my room.

What are you wearing?

My pink bathrobe. I haven't decided what to wear tonight. I'm thinking about clothing options.

---

7. Even at this early juncture I wondered which keyed the actor, physical sensation or visual memory.

What is the light like in the room?

The quality of the light in a room is tremendously evocative. The light touching our skin forms a primary boundary between I and other. We respond to light whether we know it or not. We either take it in willingly, are taken in by it, or fight its effects. In dreams light will infuse the imaginary space, setting not only the tone for a scene (as in theater lighting) but its symbolic referents. The light in my dream about Trader Jack's room was precisely that of an apartment I once lived in, and it carried with it a slew of unconscious references. Linda's answer was perfect:

Empty— like it always is.

What is your body like in the pink bathrobe in the empty light?

Itchy. I feel tense in my shoulders, dirty. I need a shower to wash the day off.

Already situated empathically with Linda, I began to experience the feel of skin against bathrobe. The pink cloth was particularly nasty, itchy, and grimy. My own simultaneous experience of her story showed me that her feelings of frustration and humiliation were brewing. The dirty, grimy feelings were physical cues to the coming event. I kept them central in our exploration. I directed Linda back and forth to the distinct image and sensations of the empty light and the grimy itchiness, paying particular attention to her skin, until she could move fluidly between them. Thus anchored, these objects symbolized the story she told herself to that point.

When does Dan arrive?

He is already late. He didn't think to ask what time to arrive so the evening would progress smoothly.

How do you know Dan has arrived?

He knocked on my door.

How do you feel when you hear his knock?

Annoyed, already angry, dirty.

Where do you feel this in your body?

In my heart and throat.

How does his face seem to you as he enters?

Fresh, glad to see me. Unaware of my feelings.

What does his fresh face look like in the empty light?

Stupid.

Where in your body do you most feel his stupid, fresh face?

When she looked at Dan in her mind's eye the sensations in her body changed. She felt as though her heart and throat had "a rope wound tightly around them." Linda reported that "this feeling, this constriction is too much." I intuitively skipped Dan's words, keeping Linda in her own body.[8]

What happens in your body as you begin to confess?

The rope loosens around my heart and throat.

---

8. It was clear to me that Linda did not need to include Dan's derogatory remarks; the tightening rope was the impetus to confess. Had I changed the focus to Dan's words I intuited two risks: that the exercise would begin with anger (a secondary emotion to shame) and that the intensity of such a controlling emotion would overwhelm the more complex scenario that she had unfolded.

Her voice was emotionally full. Her body was engaged. I asked her to move back (in her physicalized imagination) to the moment of greatest constriction. She nodded.

I then asked her to open her eyes and begin Helena's monologue.

The inescapable pressure of a perilous confession framed her work. By the end she was transformed into a martyr facing the fire. Later that day Linda performed the monologue in class. It was better and even more specific the second time without my assistance.

I meant to ask her how she prepared—what she'd done immediately before starting the monologue in class—but I forgot. Well over a year later, while readying myself to write about this experience, I emailed her and asked if she might possibly remember. She shot back this response:

> My thoughts just before doing my monologue were of my sensitive, irritated, red skin, the hollow, cold light, and Dan's face which was pinched, stubborn and unmoving. I selected these particular physicalized images just the moment before I began acting. Once the words of the monologue came out, the images disappeared as if their job were completed, making room for the words and the immediate situation I found myself in as Helena. To this day, I can still instantly trigger all of those feelings, sensations, and images.

I have asked dozens of professional actors who employ the technique of affective memory how they trigger it in performance.[9] Invariably, they will go to the autobiographical event and locate their outrage or whatever emotion it elicited. Linda's emotion was certainly present, but the environment contained it *along with* other richly re-imagined objects. The effect on her acting was textured and dense, and it

---

9. All actors are at the mercy of memory and its affects, one of which is emotion. But here I refer only to the technique of affective memory.

remained specific to the text. Most importantly, the memory became an informing environment rather than a pretext for emotion. I think (I hope) this is what Stanislavsky had in mind, even if it is not *quite* the way it transmogrified into Emotional Recall in the United States. So, at last, and pretty late in the day, I had a formal approach to making memory affective. I conducted a different experiment the following day.

Manish Goyal enters the rehearsal room vibrating with nervous excitement. He is working on Hamlet's "Oh what a rogue and peasant slave. . . ."[10] He thinks he's ready, but I am suspect of his lack of focused concentration. In the evenings he's in rehearsal as Creon for a production of Anouilh's *Medea*, and as he prepares to begin work with me, he complains and wrangles over his sense of failure and impotence in preparing the role. Working on Hamlet, a character closer to his age and experience, offers him a more manageable challenge.

As I listen, I'm struck by the fact that Manish's struggle to create a living Creon is analogous to Hamlet's dilemma in the "Oh what a rogue and peasant slave" monologue. Hamlet punishes himself for his cowardice and inaction in much the same way that Manish is punishing himself for his inability to act the part of Creon. Both are plagued by not being enough. Whether you wish to call this a substitution, as in theater, or a parallel process, as in psychology, the effect is the same. I put the analogy to Manish and ask if it has any resonance for him. The response is immediate: his dark eyes lighten, his nervous energy coalesces, his body looks ready to work—this imaginative story has ignited him. However, what would have been a fairly straightforward situational substitution exercise turns into a strange experiment.

He sits. I impulsively veer away from the substitution, and without really thinking, ask Manish instead to picture a moment in *Medea* when he can see himself acting brilliantly as Creon (the bureaucrat

---

10. *Hamlet*, act 2, scene 2.

king of Anouilh's play, saddled with grave duties and immense sovereign power). Although no such moment has actually transpired, Manish takes a second, sees an image, and nods.

What do you see?

Creon is trying to be a king and make a decision. He wants to kill Medea but can't because he's suffered too much war and killing.

Manish's response is too intellectual to be useful. But it's also perfect, since this is precisely where he's stuck as an actor. I proceed by leading Manish into contact with the sensory details of Creon's imaginative world.

What is he wearing?

An overcoat draped around his shoulders.

What kind of fabric?

Green wool.

What does his body feel like in the green wool?

Hot.

At this point, my own imagination begins to engage. Sitting in my chair in the cool rehearsal studio, I feel uncomfortably warm. There's a pause. Then Manish says,

My face is hot.

He's wearing only shorts and a soccer shirt but he's started a slight sweat. I continue:

What is he doing with his body?

Holding a cane.

What is the cane like?

Wooden with a simple curved handle.

What is his hand like holding the cane?

These questions bring Manish more fully into his sensate, imagined environment. The baffling and ungrammatical," "What is his hand like holding the cane?" bypasses any chance of Manish's giving a "right" answer. Instead, he gives the necessary one.

It's gripping it to prevent him from falling.

Why would he fall?

He feels like fainting.

What is it like, this feeling of fainting?

Medea's words are piercing him over and over.

Stay with that for a moment.

"Stay with that for a moment," in other words, feel the sensory and visual until they are fused together. This has become the most frequent prompt in our dreamwork. Manish is entering deeply into the imaginative heart of the scene. I ask:

How does his body experience this?

I hold onto my cane to keep myself from fainting. I tell myself what I must do.

Without an explicit question, Manish has made the transition from
third to first person. He is now identified with his vision. I ask him
to describe the quality of light around Creon.

> Hot, warm, yellow. The hot light of Medea is jabbing me.

We continue in this vein for several minutes more, aiming to establish the physical and imaginative reality of this "brilliantly acting
Creon."

Once Manish's body is thoroughly occupied with the physicality
of the imagery, I impulsively shift the imaginative focus of the exercise. I ask him to pull back and see himself watching this Manish-
Creon act. He seems to summon the image easily, nods, and I proceed:

> What are you wearing?
>
> A green flannel shirt with yellow stripes and jeans.
>
> What is your body doing?
>
> My hand is gripping in a fist.

His right forearm is extended downward, muscles quivering, fist
clenched. I ask about the light in this new imaginary space. Manish
replies:

> It's warm and yellow on the front of my body. . . but there's a place
> on the back of my neck where the stage light doesn't reach . . . and
> that's cold.

The spontaneity of his imagination is at play. I ask how he feels as
he watches himself playing Creon so well, and he says:

Excited. I feel it in my head. It feels like a rushing in my head. . . . It makes me want to take a deep breath.

I tell him to take that deep breath and begin the Hamlet monologue. His work was self-punishing and chilling.

What had begun as a substitution exercise took the shape of a created hallucination. We did not substitute a real-life experience for a theatrical experience of similar stripe. We created two wholly new experiences cut of purely imaginative cloth.

The case of Manish-Creon-Hamlet offers an introduction to some of the basic conceptual schemes that I'll return to in the following pages. One of the first phenomena that captured my attention while working with actors in this manner was the distinct imaginative *embodied* worlds we created through the rehearsal exercises. In Linda's case, there was a vivid, informing re-creation of her body in the landscape of her own room, but every aspect of the memory was endowed with a consciousness it did not have in life. In Manish's case we worked from the domains of memory, the present reality, and a completely fabricated experience.

By the end of our work together Manish had, in effect, three bodies. There was the rehearsal room Manish preparing to do a *Hamlet* monologue, the Manish-Creon acting brilliantly on the stage, and the Manish watching from the darkened house of the auditorium. Each body had a physical life (dressed in his own wardrobe) and a psychic life, and each was observable by the others. Each body inhabited its own, distinct landscape, but was bound in a mutually affective relationship with the other two Manishes. This peculiar imaginative interdependence would later become an important aspect of the dreamwork.

But what this early work made clear me was that the boundaries of the body are able to exchange and contribute sensory information not merely in the present world, but in any world inhabited by a sentient body. We made the body sentient by exploring its sensations, however imagined. An actor re-inhabiting a memory had actually been there, but a dreamer inhabiting a dream had actually been there as well. All that was required for our purposes was a sentient body. If Manish could embody an experience that was constructed by us both in the moment, then by extension, it should be relatively easy to bring the waking actor's body back into the landscape of a richly imagined dream.

Why, however, did the fabricated body of Manish acting beautifully as Creon work for the purposes of *Hamlet*? I suspected that this body offered Manish a perspective and state he had not previously known. And I wondered if this effective man, this king, was the missing piece, the ultimate aspiration of both Manish and Hamlet. When sensately anchored as an aspect of the whole he served as both what was necessary and what was sorely absent.

The experiments with Linda and Manish led to my first attempt at connecting actual dreams with acting—an attempt that was inelegant and grossly comical.

In a beginning scene study class I inquired if everyone had recently dreamt and retained a dream in memory. Then, like the Reverend Sun Yung Moon conducting mass arranged weddings, I led the whole class simultaneously through their dream landscapes. It was an extremely messy business. I then asked the students to go around in a circle and act their monologues—which had no explicit connection to these dreams—allowing themselves to be affected by the environment of the dream and the images that they experienced. I gave no other directive—nor indeed could I, for I didn't know what I was talking about. That their work was informed by powerful sources was clear. Effort and false images of acting dissipated and all of their the work seemed encompassed by a different ether, a different atmosphere. And to my amazement each actor (except one) found the process fluid and expressed the opinion that implementing the dream material was easier than using affective memory—not necessarily more appropriate, but easier. Given my own dicey history with affective memory I did not find this particularly surprising in my class. But many of these actors had studied before with Michael Ouellette, a sensitive master of affective memory, so I felt encouraged. If launching embodied images from unrelated dreams was easy and *affective*, then what might happen to the acting if the dreams were consonant with the actor and the material?

Armed with the certainty that we were on to something, I knew it was time to step firmly onto that terra incognita. After I reported these initial experiments to Robert Bosnak and Arthur Roberts, we laid the plans for taking a company of actors through a process whereby they would all generate dreams on a given play. How we might use these dreams, or be used by them, and how they would affect the creative process we did not know.

CHAPTER THREE

The Pilgrimage
to the Temple

How do you provoke dreams on a play? In the background were much larger questions. By what method would the actor "use" the dream imagery? Would the experiment result in a reliable process capable of generating desired effects? And what, specifically, might those effects be?

I sought a scheme that made sense to me and allowed the actors to feel that their work was contained within a sound, tangible structure. Robert suggested beginning with an ancient practice that he had adapted for use with his patients. It seems that twenty-five hundred years ago the priests at the Temple of Aesculapius practiced medicinal "dream incubation" on the ailing Greeks who journeyed there to be healed. It worked like this. A sick man or woman traveled to a temple. Fear of death could not have changed much over the millennia, so it's safe to assume that by the time his local physician had failed him and he felt compelled to make this pilgrimage, he was worried. Once there, he was instructed to make sacrifices and give prayers. He slept in the temple overnight, and in the morning the priest inquired into his dreams. The prescribed remedy was based on his dream images: dream homeopathy.[1]

Our interest, however, was not in curing disease but in directly exposing the actor to the fertility of her imagination. Robert and I were both pressed for time, and we decided I would be the first subject of an incubation for artists even though I am a director and all of our thinking had been focused on actors. We just wanted to see if it would work. By the same token, neither of us actually knew what "working" would look like or feel like. In a hurried session Robert and I prepared an "incubation image" together.

An incubation image is comprised of a short series of discrete images derived from the scene under examination. The idea is to first explore the images and couple them to the emergent sensate information found in the body. Then we extract these fused sensate images from the scene and make certain the subject can move easily from one to another; in other words, she can easily call up the image and the physical sensations it evoked. She then recalls them fully (as an image wed to an embodied state) for twenty seconds before sleeping in order to catalyze a response in the dreams that follow.

Robert and I cast about for a place to start. Composer John Harbison and I were kicking around the idea of collaborating on a chamber opera he had written years ago, *A Full Moon in March*, based on Yeats's play of the same name. I was honored to be asked, and looked forward to working with him. Twenty years earlier I'd directed the play, loved the myth and the verse, and had always considered

---

1. In the earliest days of the aesculapia, the patient simply dreamt. If he received a dream in which the god appeared, he was considered cured. In other words, the dream was the cure. The earliest priests were selected for the year from the citizenry, and served their terms with no special training. Some scholars consider the later intervention of the priests, via interpretation and applied cure, to be a degradation of the temples' original functioning.

revisiting it as a theater piece. This would be my first opera, but I felt
my confidence slightly bolstered by my knowledge of the play.

John gave me the libretto he'd adapted from the play, along with
a recording done years ago. One sunny afternoon, I lay down in my
office and reread the Yeats play. It still spoke to me. The gruesome,
fertile destiny of the Swineherd and the Queen, bound together,
fated by their flaws and their opposition was a myth I could dwell in
for a long while. Casually checking on the unfolding narrative in the
play, I noted all of the major turning points in the action. Then I put
the cassette on and turned to the libretto. John had cut about eight
lines from the Yeats's text, but these were the lines most meaningful
to me! Furthermore, in these cuts he excised the major turning point
in the action, the event that advances the myth as I understood it.

John and I met the following week and I harangued him as if I
possessed *the only* interpretation of this mythic play. "The action is so
spare that by cutting these lines you make the character of the Queen
implacable. And by cutting the moment when he regains his memory,
you take away the Queen's shock and the Swineherd's delight that he
is low and base, not because he's got amnesia and is mad, but because
he really is low and base, and will gladly drag her down with him!
There is no possible recourse left to her except 'off with his head,'
which is precisely what the Queen orders."

I admire John Harbison very much. His response to me was better
than I deserved. (I say this now as I write by way of apologizing for
assuming I knew what Yeats was after. I did not say it at the time.)
"You're right," he said. "I don't even want to think about what I was
thinking back then when I cut the libretto!" Then he talked about what
the piece meant to him. It was a myth of artists and implacable muses.
The music and libretto were completely consistent with the theme.

This is, most likely, what Yeats was after—after all.

John wanted to remount this opera for the pleasure of conducting it and getting a good recording. I wanted to work with John. No

problem there. Still, I was stuck with the problem of love: my love for
the Queen and a desire to re-infuse her with dimensionality. I knew
the singers would need masks in order to honor John's interpretation
of the myth,[2] but I craved the human dimension of faces. There was
no question of mutating the opera back into the play I'd loved in *my*
imagination; John's music was telling a very different tale, and that
was the narrative that needed to be told.

This seemed like a good place to start with Robert. We developed an incubation image based on the missing lines. In one line I
"saw" the Queen amused by the Swineherd, which was a relaxed place
to enter *A Full Moon in March*. Robert began.

> What are her arms like?
>
> Feminine. Intelligent. Ironic.
>
> What are they doing?

Sitting in a chair opposite Robert, I was unselfconsciously holding
my arms out in the "Queen's" manner and moving them as she did in
my mind's eye.

> They are sensing the air. Sensing the situation. Sensing herself and
> her amusement.
>
> What is happening in her body because of her arms?
>
> They form a triangle comprised of her heart, her mind, and her
> arms. They are the organs of her intelligence.
>
> What do they say?

---

2. Yeats also calls for masks in the text.

They tell me that I can remain detached. He threatens my ability to perceive.

Like Manish, I unself-consciously shift into a first person narrative. The Queen's point of view has become my own.

What happens if you join with him?

I lose myself.

An image of a village idiot appears in my mind's eye. I know it is the face of Jeanne d'Arc without the informing intelligence of her angelic voices.

What is happening in your body as you join with him?

The blood drains from my arms, my heart. It centers in my groin. I am an idiot—devoid of perception.

The incubation image was drawn from these embodied visions: the Queen's intelligent, amused arms, and joining with the Swineherd as the blood drains from my/her arms and heart.

An incubation image is far more than a summary of a scene's content and conflict. In effect, it poses a question to the autonomous imagination, and the imagination responds in similar language—with the images of dreams. The more seemingly irreconcilable the question, the greater the ingenuity and delight in the imaginative response. A purely surface understanding of these two images is that this is the Queen in two conflicting states, both of which comprise her. Fathomless questions are, "who, why, and what is she composed of in these states?" All of these questions were present in the incubation image. This is the stuff of her myth and my own.

The dream material volleyed back to me as a result of the incubation image amazed me with its relevance and precision. There was a scene about creative negotiations with John (actually two John Harbisons, one female, one male, who both looked an awful lot like him); one about creating masks; and one in which a crescent moon shaped piece had been excised from a penis. (In the verse, the Queen is associated with the moon. She has the Swineherd's head cut off. His blood then impregnates her.) All of these dream fragments were rich and informing. The second, which I will recount, was less personally revealing and directly addressed one of my directorial concerns.

In the dream, Michael Ouellette had just finished conducting a mask-making workshop (which was a lengthy dream sequence) and said, "Oh, by the way, let's just stop in here at my new house. I want your opinion about something." He opened the door to his home, and there was a nineteenth-century opera house. Beautiful! Michael said, "See that chandelier?" It was enormous; you couldn't miss it. "Where do you think I should hang it?" I was at a loss. You could hang it anywhere, and the obvious place would have been the central ceiling to show it off. I was not being asked for the obvious, however, but was being called upon for an informed, creative insight. My friend Hugo was standing behind Michael. A fast, pragmatic problem solver, Hugo looked at me as if to say, "Hang it anywhere—it doesn't matter. Make a mistake and how big a mistake would it be? It's gorgeous." Then suddenly I looked over at house right at a long, ornate opera box draped with sumptuous curtains. If the chandelier were hung there it would dwarf the space in a really challenging and confrontational way—very fresh.

When I went back into that part of the dream as an embodied landscape (whose process I will discuss at length later) I saw that in order to re-introduce to the production the intimacy necessary to me as a director I could close the performance space in, setting the size of the music against a dwarfed, more pressurized, mythic environment. Bingo! I had the beginnings of a conceptual approach. This first, hurried attempt at connecting an artist and a play proved to be a problem-solving bonanza.

All of the steps we took offered information. The incubation image yielded a physical manifestation the Queen could use, those intelligent arms (just right for a singer). The image and the incubated dream furnished the terrible and magnificent consequences of the Swineherd's and Queen's actions. They were now encoded in physicalized sensation, available for my use as a director.

The idiot Jeanne d'Arc and the excised penis were entirely new to me; they were products of an imagination to which I did not have conscious access. I received their meaning, understood their relevance, and made certain concrete directorial decisions based upon them. But they were so complex and complete that I knew I could never use them up, nor could I completely understand them. They both contained symbolic mystery for me that, even now as I write, remains frightening and eloquent. The images were easily employed, but they also filled me with awe. They represented the most intimate connections between the text and me, the ones I'd endeavor to direct, never *quite* knowing what it was that was trying to express itself through me. I've accepted the fact that, although most of a director's work is conscious and intentional, some things manifest onstage that she did not quite intend consciously, as if the work were a couple of years ahead of consciousness. The dreamwork brought these to consciousness and made me feel that I was years ahead of the game, while at the same time knowing that I did not know all the rules. And how could I? The dream had woven for me a personally analogous myth out of Yeats's Swineherd and Queen, and as we all know, myths reveal themselves endlessly in layers or they wouldn't be myths.

This is a wonderful position for a director to find herself in, but I wanted something else for actors. I wanted the dreams to carry the actors' performances into a new sphere of imagination as they acted. Encouraged by the ease of generating momentous dreams explicitly connected to dramatic material Robert and I set out to re-configure the priests' scheme for our purposes with actors.

The rationale at the Temple of Aesculapius was that the God collaborated best with the patient himself. It was he who had the most extensive and intimate knowledge of his ailment and the greatest stake in finding its cure. Through dreams the God infused him with an inspired remedy. We took this model and shifted it to suit the theater. Our plan was to work with a group of actors in a workshop. We would prepare incubation images from the scenes they were rehearsing and then ask them to recall these embodied images in the hopes of seeding their dreams. Who knew better what was needed than the actor herself? Our hope was that a collaboration with the Gods—which is to say, with the realms of an actor's imagination—would yield inspired results.

Ritual—such as the one at the aesculapium at Epidaurus—evolves within a specific cultural context that plays an important role in its effectiveness. In designing our experiment for incubating actors' dreams, we analyzed the factors that supported healing at the temple and then translated these into the cultural context of contemporary theater. These were the fundamental conditions we understood as important:[3]

- The actor, like the fearful patient, must be emotionally engaged.

- In place of the patient's offerings and prayers, an equivalent preparatory process must take place that serves to dedicate the actor completely to the task at hand.

---

3. These represent our initial criteria, and they still hold up for the most part. As the book progresses, I introduce other approaches that factor into creating both incubation images and the dreamworked body. The final chapter will summarize those choices we still use.

- The incubation image should be comprised of contrasting or opposing images or states, just as the ailing man held hopes for health and fear of illness in the same state.

- The dreamworker would stand in for the priest, working homeopathically by using the actor's words and visions as the "treatment" for generating dreams.

Let me clarify this last point. One of our underlying assumptions is that dreams are a product of the imagination, and that imagination is by its very nature intelligent and playful. We assumed that if we addressed the imagination homeopathically, in its own language, it would respond in kind. Dreams are imaginative imagery, so we would seed them with imaginatively engendered visual images. We hoped the actors' dreams would rebound with a depth of creativity that the reflexive or constructive imaginations alone could not supply. To say it simply: if the actor presents a charged image directly to her imagination, her imagination will playfully do *something* with that image. And that something is likely to be far more profound and surprising than anything she could willfully invent.

CHAPTER FOUR

Prayers and
Offerings

I convened an experimental workshop comprised of Robert Bosnak, Arthur Roberts, a group of talented young actors, and me.[1] The plan was to work on scenes from Chekhov's *The Seagull*, and we would meet weekly to conduct our experiment. I worried about everything. Would taking their work into their dreams prove too exhausting? Are people *supposed* to work in their sleep? Would intensive exploration of dream material be a rattling experience? Would the whole experiment fail to yield anything productive? Accustomed to worrying, I proceeded as if I weren't.

We spent several sessions analyzing *The Seagull* for its content, structure, and rhythms. This period served as part of our preliminary prayers and offerings and, as such, was essential to the work that came later. Discovering the cruelty and humor; the characters' vagaries,

---

1. The actors were Linda Tsang, Tara Perry, Charles Armesto, Monica Gomi, Manish Goyal, and Fernando Paiz.

drives, and desires; the parallel relationships; and the contrapuntal nature of the scenes and acts enabled everyone to make personal connections to the material and to experience the play as a unified whole. Moreover, it widened the field of experience to include everyone in the group in pursuit of the answers to the existential questions posed (and left largely unresolved) by this great play.

Poring over *The Seagull*'s exquisite and poignant changes in subjects, and then asking and answering why things were said and done was not left to the individual alone. Each person heard the insights of the others, however unpleasant they seemed, and the vying points of view expanded the field. Nina is gladly seduced by a narcissist, and Linda, who was cast in that role, listened to the dark comprehension of a narcissist's self-love and secret self-loathing discussed by the older adult men in the room. In a revolutionary moment Robert suggested that Treplev was already seeking his death at the beginning of act 2 and the actors rebelled. This psychoanalytical perspective violated their understanding of dramatic structure. If Treplev is seeking his own death at the beginning of act 2 then the actor would be playing the end of the play before the middle, and every student of Stanislavsky knows you cannot do that! Right or wrong, the profundity of Treplev's self-destruction was sown in their minds. At another point I rather nastily attacked Nina's character, and Linda strenuously objected, "I've had enough! She's a sweet, lovely girl!" (Linda's acting proved me wrong in the end.) We had a thrilling time together; it doesn't get much better than being in the presence of a great play with a group of exceptionally smart, dedicated people. And while we argued and reflected aloud, we introduced a world of possibilities into the wider field of communal perception that could not be retracted.

On the practical level, these nights of traditional text analysis gave us the time to get everyone dreaming and recording his or her dreams. Two weeks later we had a group of dreaming actors, and we began developing the incubation images, the keys that would, perhaps, prompt germane dreams on *The Seagull*.

These early incubation processes were simple but delicate.[2] Our first step is to ask the actor, "Which moment in the scene do you find most compelling?" Or alternatively, "Which moment most disgusts you, most fascinates, or excites?" Or, "Which moment do you find the most upsetting or the most intriguing?" Like the ailing Greek patient consumed by health concerns, the actor is already captivated by something delightful in the scene or a problem he's gnawing over. After giving time for the actor to locate the moment in his minds eye, we ask him, "What do you see?"

Because our intent is to engage the imagination, we specifically do not ask, "What do you imagine?" Asking an actor to imagine places him under pressure. He may well fear he won't imagine well enough. And we all know that imagination does not respond to force: the faster you run after it, the faster it recedes, like trying to catch your shadow. Volitional acts always carry the potential for perceived failure. On the other hand we feel that seeing simply happens to us— we *just* see—while imagining is something we must do. In asking, "What do you see?" we implicitly tell the actor that he is already having a concrete experience the likes of which he has every day and in every waking moment. Even if he had no visual image in mind, he'll spontaneously comply by producing something to see that he can then report to us. One last point before I return to the story. We tend to regard imagination as atemporal, which makes us feel that it takes place outside of our subjective sense of time. Sensation, on the other

---

2. The early incubation images were all prepared sequentially, the simplest technique, rather than simultaneously. (see Chapter 9 and Conclusion.)

hand, feels as though it's happening right now; in fact, it *is* happening right now. Seeing is a precise, immediate action that we know occurs in the present—the best place for an actor to be. And of course, once we engage our sense of sight it simultaneously places us in a landscape that can be further embodied.

And so with that question, "What do you see?" we prepare our first incubation image for *The Seagull*. Linda is playing Nina in the scene with Treplev in act 2 and told us that the moment in the scene that most compels her is the moment Treplev lays the seagull at Nina's feet.

What do you see?

Linda describes the image that manifests itself spontaneously:

> She [Nina] sits on a bench in a long dress. It's sunny. She looks at the landscape—which is beautiful. Suddenly, something makes her look down, and there is a dead seagull and a pair of muddy shoes.

Robert will patiently tease out the strands of this brief anecdote until it becomes a sentient environment. He will slowly and deliberately fuse together the visual, physical, and emotional. Willingness on the part of the questioner to be empathically present in the actor's unfolding experience is essential. By discretely joining the field of experience, he senses his way through his own body. This stimulates his imagination and gives him the ability to negotiate the landscape. The importance of this rapport shouldn't be underestimated. I suppose it is theoretically possible that the technique could yield results even if the questioner were not attuned to the actor's experience, but I doubt that it's possible in practice. First of all, the process the questioner and actor engage in together puts the actor in a receptive state not unlike the hypnagogic state we experience as we fall asleep.

Finally, the sensitivity involved increases the actor's sense of safety and trust.[3]

After several minutes of patient questioning, Linda arrived at this expanded first-person vision.

> The sun is on my face. It's warm. I see myself in a dress that covers my shoes. I can't really see my shoes or legs at all. My clothing is wholly inappropriate for the weather. I should have brought my wrap. I should have known better . . . I hear my mother's voice saying that I should have known better.

While Nina's mother is dead, Linda's mother is not. She is a vibrant presence in Linda's life.

> I'm cold and shivering. I'm trying to have a little contact with the bench for warmth . . . My back is really stiff. It's stiffening up. I'm so cold, so stiff. My back feels like steel . . . I look out at the grass and trees. They are beautiful. Then I look down. I don't know why—I didn't hear a sound. There is the seagull. For some reason I really want to see some blood—but I don't see any blood. The seagull looks almost alive; its feathers are only dirty from the mud. Its wings are deformed. Then I look

---

3. No actor will go beyond his resistances without the faith that he will either be guided back, or can find his way back, from extremity. Gestalt psychotherapists Erving and Miriam Polster write, "If one really fears that his silliness will turn into hebephrenic permanence or that if he were to cry, he would cry forever, he would surely be wise to block out silliness and crying . . . The necessary support for exploring these mini-madnesses may come from several directions . . . like the Yogi who needs a companion when he goes into the depths of his non-being lest someone cart him off for dead." Erving Polster and Miriam Polster, Gestalt Therapy Integrated (New York: Brunner/Mazel, 1973), 203–204.

at its eye. There is only one eye staring up at me, and it's like a black marble. Beady. Now I see the top half of a man's muddy shoes. They are Treplev's.

Linda's imagined vision reached its organic end point at Treplev's muddy shoes. Distilling a clear and concise incubation image is the next step, and it brings this part of the process to a close.

Still deeply focused, Linda was asked to sequentially re-experience the following sensations that comprise the fully formed incubation image: (1) the chilly feeling in her back—"like cold steel making contact with the bench" (2) the sight of the seagull's dead, "marble"-like, "beady" eye and (3) the sight of the "muddy" shoes. When she was able to move effortlessly from one of these points to another, the process was complete.

Linda will recall these three reference points and experience all of their sensual parts for twenty to thirty seconds prior to going to sleep each night until our next meeting. And she will record her dreams.

The Gods Speak

When we met for the next session Linda reported that she'd had several dreams, but none were related to the incubation image. When pressed, she said that one of the dreams was about her family but it was saturated with images from a book called *Wild Swans*,[4] which I had lent to her a few weeks earlier. I asked her to tell a little of this dream even though she felt it had no relevance to Nina or to the play in general. Linda said,

It was a dream about a woman with bound feet. There were these dirty strips of white rag binding them. And the feet were—unimag-

---

4. Jung Chang, *Wild Swans: Three Daughters of China* (New York: Anchor, 1991).

inably—three inches long! I stared at her feet. How could anybody's feet—and she was thirty-five years old—be three inches long? And I remember wanting to go down to the ground to see their size. I couldn't believe it.

The relevance of this dream to Linda-as-Nina was plain to Arthur, Robert, and me. The central metaphor for Linda's understanding of Nina was given by the dream: Nina's feet are bound. In the beginning of the play they're bound by her father and stepmother, but even after the action runs its course, when she returns to Sorin's estate in the final act, they are still bound. Only now they're bound by Trigorin, Treplev, the estate on the lake, the theater—and by the very future that she sought as escape from her bound past. But Linda hadn't yet consciously arrived at this understanding of Nina's arc through the play. After recounting her entire dream once through, she said, "See? This was about my family and that book!" It only took Robert's pointing out that Nina, too, has a family, to persuade Linda to continue. The two of them started on the next stage of the process.

Robert began.

Are you sitting or standing?

Standing.

How are you standing?

I am standing erect. Just as if I were walking down the street and I suddenly stopped.

Is the awareness of the woman's feet sudden or gradual?

It's kind of gradual. I stop and see her face. She has a lovely face, round and oval. . . . A very pleasing smile, very contagious. She's wearing a beautifully rich dress: Chinese silk, red, with a pattern of phoenixes and dragons.

Is this a period costume?

Yes. It's extremely expensive. I glance at the pattern on the garment and my eyes travel down.

How is she holding her head?

She is holding her head very tall, very proud. Very confident.

Can you feel the proud confidence with which she is holding her head?

Linda experiences this and nods. At Robert's suggestion, she has made a transition into the dream character's body. He continues:

How is it in her back?

It is straight but it's very relaxed.

How is it in her stomach?

Kind of tight. Like she's holding it in.

Feel her balance.

She's slightly wavering, but it's not perceivable just from looking.

You can feel the slight wavering?

Linda nods.

How are her legs?

They are straight and together. Like she wasn't walking. Like she was standing.

Are they pressed together?

Yes, they are.

Can you feel that?

Uh huh.

And what is she feeling in her feet?

Linda is silent and intensely emotional. Robert continues after a
pause.

What happens when all of the attention is focused in her feet?

I am begging for the pain to stop.

Linda has adopted the first-person voice, transiting naturally into the
character.

And with this feeling, what is it like for Nina to see the seagull?

I want it to go away.

How does it affect your posture and movements?

I become very still. I'm shaking a little. Twitching.

Where do you feel that twitch?

In my face.

Next, Robert draws Linda's attention to the scene in *The Seagull,* a
movement I will discuss later.

Are you looking at the seagull?

Uh huh.

Keep looking at the seagull and see what happens. . . .

There is a long pause during which there is a fierce, concentrated silence.

What has happened?

I am losing my balance on the bench.

What is it like to be so off-balance on that bench?

Another long pause. This time Linda's body stiffens.

What is happening to your right fist?

I'm trying to hold on to something—but there is nothing to hold on to.

Linda's right fist was tightly clenched, her face was pale, and she was holding her breath. Robert gently reminded her to breathe and to keep focusing on her breath as she returned to the presence of the room in which we sat.

When he asked, "Are you looking at the seagull?" Robert employed a particular kind of hypnotic suggestion called a conversational postulate to encourage Linda to look at the seagull—ostensibly in the hopes of fusing Linda's dream imagery with the imagery of the play. This choice felt wrong to me. It was intrusive. It was at this moment that Linda fell into a protracted silence, blanched, and held in her breath. Even I experienced coercion when Robert shifted the questions in this way. If the incubated dream is the actor's link to the play, I felt that it was unnecessary to force a more explicit connection to the play's imagery. Injecting our desire to create an overt connection to the play felt like mixing apples and oranges. The chillingly perfect imagery given by the dream should be enough. We decided to omit this maneuver in our next round of incubation.[5]

Let's step back and look at Linda's situation in context.

Linda, an Asian American woman playing Nina, states that the most compelling moment in her scene is when Treplev lays the seagull at Nina's feet. After creating an incubation image based on that moment, she dreams that she is watching with nauseated fascination as an Asian woman bears the unbearable—three-inch-long bound feet—with pain and pride. Consider Nina's famous line in act 4: "I am a seagull. No, that's not right. I am an actress." Could there be a line that is more difficult for an actor to bring to life than, "I am a seagull?" The words have such impossible metaphorical meaning—and she must say them so many times during that scene! It's an actor's bête noire.

Linda's incubation image acted as a question to her imagination, and her imagination responded with a metaphor pregnant with personal meaning. What's more, in transforming Chekhov's metaphor—the seagull—into an analogous one, Linda's imagination made it possible for her to comprehend the symbolic structure of Nina's dilemma. The dream of the bound feet generated a gravid metaphor whose effects were threefold: Linda now understood the event of act

---

5. A year later, armed with a great deal of expertise and faith that only experience can yield, we began fusing all sorts of complex connections in both the dream imagery and the incubation imagery. More on this in a later chapter, but it is worth mentioning here. However, we maintained the purity of the dreamwork by never re-introducing the actor's history, the play, or the incubation. The later variations pull together more complex threads that would be distracting at this point. Finally, and this is crucial, the actor's ability to have faith in the process and to experience it without force or pressure is directly linked to the dreamworker's ease. As our expertise increased, the process grew more comfortable, and much shorter as well. Our confidence in bringing new issues into the mix felt right to us and we did it without effort. In these early days we were still feeling our way through.

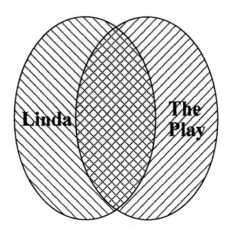

4; she personally identified with Nina's particular dilemma; and she had a conscious and empathic sense of Nina's throughline in the play.

We forged a direct link between the imagination of the actor and the imagination of the playwright. Linda's dream images were densely charged with intimate personal significance because they were hers, and with relevant meaning because of the interpenetration of her imagination and the imagination of the play. The red of the dream dress, the soiled bindings, the dimensions of the feet—these were all specific images emerging from the overlap of Linda's imagination and the play's imagination. They whispered their meaning into her being. How sumptuous! Each imaginative stroke is simultaneously *of* the play and awash with personal, emotional relevance for the actor.

The shaded area in the figure can be attributed to neither Linda nor The Play alone. It's inevitably a product of them both. An imaginative story sprang forth at a redrawn boundary. First we widened the field of experience to include Linda and The Play by virtue of the incubation image, which placed them both firmly in the same environment. This sensitivity at the newly created boundary invited a high degree of expression of autonomous imagination. Linda's dreams then created new metaphors that gave voice to this newly sensitized boundary. The dream gave Linda the powerful metaphor. Reinhabiting the dream landscape gave her the means to experience the metaphor sensually. So far so good.

Unfortunately, we had no idea how to apply so potent an image to the actual work of performing the scene.

CHAPTER FIVE

The God Is Silent;
The God Speaks

The Dionysian implications of this work were challenging, alarming, and alluring. The possibility of addressing Artaud's aesthetic demands for ecstatic acting with an organic model held tremendous attraction. Could we bypass the actor's conscious mind and go right to "unconscious acting" by trusting the dreams alone? What would happen if we refrained from employing any consciously applied structural framework, like physical actions, objectives, and activities? Robert maintained that such concepts grew out of a mechanistic model of human behavior—remnants of the obsolete nineteenth-century notion that we are essentially rational beings who behave in accordance with certain objectives that we determine. If that were the case then the dreamwork presented the possibility of a nonmechanistic approach, Quantum Acting!

I considered Robert's proposal for an wholly organic, ecstatic method. If acting is sacred to the God Dionysus, and the work of the actor is to invite the God into his body, then action is based on the infusion of the God into human form. In true Dionysian fashion all characters should be in the grip of implacable necessity—in other words, "out of their minds." Perhaps rehearsing in the traditional conscious ways would militate against this infusion. Yet, as a card-carrying member of Stanislavsky's objectives and actions, I doubted that actors who lacked the structure of the scene imprinted in their moving bodies could succeed. Acting is both a machine and a miracle, and one mechanistic process catalyzes countless connections. Also, in some fundamental way, actors (and designers and directors) re-learn their art in the context of every production. The gestalt of the play requires time in rehearsal to interact with the artist. After arguing against Robert's proposal in every way I could, what harm was there in trying the "New Organic Dionysian Method?" I mean, what if it worked? That would really be something.

In every good experiment the groups need to be controlled: Group A takes the placebo, Group B takes nothing, Group C takes the experimental drug. Heigh-ho to responsible experimentation! We abandoned Groups A and B entirely. Here was the opportunity to see what our Group C would do. They, the Dionysian Group, would simply "act from the dreams." I'll recount these early attempts briefly because they yielded important insights, but it won't be pleasant. Those first experiences in putting the images to work were aesthetically and emotionally painful for the actors and for me. Nevertheless, they taught us an enormous amount about the process and about the potency of the dreamwork.

We proceeded directly from the incubated dream images to the actual scenes. The actors quickly re-inhabited their most potent dream images briefly before starting. Then they performed the scenes. The results were dismal. The dreams subverted the acting. If in the dream the actor could not move, then in the scene she remained rooted to the spot—literally unable to wrench herself out of her position—regardless of what the other actor was doing. This was no trivial phenomenon. I chose these actors because they were adept at responding in the moment to present stimuli. But there they were, disabled, incapable of reacting spontaneously to anything but the force of the dream. It exerted more influence than did the consensual reality in which the scene needed to take place.

We were all pretty devastated. Morale was low for everyone except Robert, whose buoyant optimism was a tonic. I knew we needed to regroup, but frankly, the only thing I could think to do at this point was rehearse and try launching the dreams later. Robert offered support for this solution in Jung's discussion of the "alchemical vas."

The alchemical opus is often represented symbolically as a cooking process: its rooms are the kitchen and the laboratory. Different elements (whether conceived as salt and lead, analyst and analysand, or ensemble and text) are thrown together in a large pot, the lid is put on, the fire is lit, and the stew begins to simmer. But as the elements start to percolate and blend together in the alchemical pot, the pressure of their transformation must be contained. A weak vessel will crack, and a cracked one will leak. To guard against this, the pot must be well made, well prepared, and well maintained. The vas is this sturdy vessel that contains and supports the disparate elements placed within it and allows their transformation to occur. Maintaining the integrity of the vessel must take precedence over any other aspect of transformational work—be that work alchemical, psychotherapeutic, or theatrical.

Working from this analogy, our experiment had proceeded thus far without the necessary safety afforded by the presence of a sturdy, encompassing vas. We needed to tend to our vessel, and we went about it in fairly traditional fashion: we rehearsed. I worked each scene twice before our next laboratory session. The actors made genuine contact with one another and took time finding and inhabiting the moments. They made specific choices, embodied their actions, and moved toward throughlines that gave the scenes shape and content.

But another story will serve to further this narrative more clearly. It's the story of an incubated dream that had surprising and remarkable effects that helped crystallize our understanding of the entire process.

The God Speaks

Tara Perry—the actor who instigated my thinking about dreamwork and imagination—was playing Arkadina in the scene with Trigorin in act 3. She struggled with her role during two weeks of rehearsal. It lacked the depth and subtlety that usually marks her work. Several acting issues were at play. Tara was in her early twenties and had little of Arkadina's experience of life, sexuality, or manipulation. The desperation, love, betrayal, and abandonment Arkadina experiences in this crisis with Trigorin were never minted in Tara's adult life. Her approach was to return to the memory of a childhood love and the subsequent betrayal at the hands of this friend—hoping to mine that emotional upheaval. But Tara's autobiographical scenario wasn't capable of reaching the level of nuance and desperation that drives Arkadina's action in the scene. There was one other significant issue. An impasse arose in her work with the actor playing Trigorin who had no difficulty being sexually manipulative in the scene. Although Tara had worked well with him many times before, this time she found him distasteful and unseemly. And though these feelings could rightly find their way into that complex scene, they were hamstringing Tara's acting.

We discussed these issues outside of rehearsal. Tara envisioned that if she personalized the scene in a new way she might transcend her difficulties. She came up with the absurdly wonderful substitution that the actor playing Trigorin was asking her to change scene partners. She imagined that he wanted to act with Linda (who played Nina) because she was a better actress, more sensitive, more emotionally connected, and more sensual. I then suggested that she re-imagine the words of the text so that they would regain their seminal meaning, a technique that Tara often uses successfully. Working on her own she began finding an inroad to Arkadina's sense of entitlement that allows her to behave with such high drama.

By the time we presented the scene to the group Tara transformed her acting. She swept onstage with the manipulative majesty of a great actor—Arkadina, in fact. Trigorin was given no quarter. Tara managed to allow a perceptible loosening of Arkadina's mask, and we glimpsed the terrible, desperate risks she was forced to take. The scene was funny while being in deadly earnest—a fitting tone for *The Seagull*. She had worked through her difficulties with talent, invention, style, and theatricality. It was wonderful, and I thought that I couldn't be happier. But the next two events conspired to show me the immense possibilities that lay beneath the mask of acting.

After the scene had run through once and we all expressed our admiration, we conducted an experiment. We asked Tara to work with Robert in re-evoking the landscape of a particular dream she'd had several weeks before, and then to launch directly into the scene again. The incubation image for that dream had been drawn from the moment when Trigorin tells Arkadina that "something draws him" to Nina, and he asks her to let him go. Tara brought back the following dream fragment: She is in a dark, abandoned warehouse. Her arms are thrust behind her body, pressing against a desk with her hands. A man—who never quite comes into focus—kneels in front of her. Sensing his fear of her provokes little electric shocks along her skin. Her body is erect, as if she were corseted. She feels wild and abandoned.

When we'd done the Group C Dionysian experiment, launching this dream on the scene had failed miserably. Now, after two weeks of rehearsal, Tara and Robert worked together to re-evoke the dream and anchor its imagery in her body. Tara refrained from making up any details that she couldn't actually recall. As they worked, she felt her weight shifted back onto her hands, the darkness of the warehouse, the dim light from the window, and, finally, the presence of the man who seemed to fear her and whose fear evoked the little shocks on her skin. After five minutes of this, Tara was deeply involved with the dream images and their corresponding sensations. Her eyes were closed and she seemed connected to these new currents in her body. At this point, I asked Tara to open her eyes, take in the rehearsal room "with the gaze of this body," and begin the scene.[1]

The work that followed was electrifying; but more importantly, it was revelatory. Tara's body underwent a radical transformation. An asymmetrical torque canted her hips and upper body and produced a bizarre leaning carriage. Throughout the scene, her hands gestured in unaccountable ways, seemingly of their own accord. Their motion was neither spastic nor wasteful; each unexpected movement supported Arkadina's words and behavior, and then cleared new paths through which they could manifest. The gesticulating hands were like living symbols, dense with meaning yet irreducible. In Tara's retrospective account, she reported experiencing electrical shocks throughout her body. She had been acutely aware of her body in its every movement. She felt she had no reason to override these; her body seemed to be "working according to its own necessity." From her inner perspective, as well as our outer one, it seemed that this Tara-Arkadina struggled for ownership of Trigorin's weakening body, and surpassed his sexuality.

I can best describe the overall effect as a kind of visitation. A terribly real person—terrible in her desperation and utterly, completely alive, inhabited Tara. She was an actor possessed by Dionysus. The

---

1. "With the gaze of this body" has proven an unnecessary prompt. We now simply have actors recall and reinhabit the dreamworked body (the images derived from the dreams) for a few seconds before making an entrance, and then let go of it.

dreamwork evoked a divine body that echoed but didn't exactly replicate the body in Tara's dream. None of us had ever seen her inhabit such a body before. In fact, in all my years of teaching, I've not seen such a thorough, seemingly cellular transformation occur in any actor.

A veil was lifted from acting itself. The scene's throughline remained, but its conventional buttresses—the narrative markers of articulated objectives and action—disappeared. All effort on the part of the actor vanished. All self-censorship dissolved. A living woman remained who revealed that which is only shown in life in private moments. The crisis of Trigorin's attempted defection catalyzed a complete and desperately divided identity. Her speech and behavior made painfully clear that what she was consciously intending she was unconsciously sabotaging. The demons that lay beneath Arkadina's social mask glared through its cracks. I was reminded of Budd Schulman's description of Sammy Glick's expression in *What Makes Sammy Run*, as he watched his first screen credit appear, "There is no word in English to describe it. . . . I felt it was something I should not be allowed to see, like the face of the boy who roomed across the hall from me in prep school when I made the sordid mistake of entering without knocking." We entered without knocking and saw Arkadina, a woman in crisis, a house divided, a neurotic, in short, a mess. But she was a shockingly powerful, completely unyielding, and entirely specific mess.

A story about Olympia Dukakis might highlight the difference between Tara's first and second takes on the scene. I loved Olympia's gloriously architectural, energized acting of the 1970s and '80s. She mastered the imaginative and fully inhabited action in pursuit of her objective. Her work changed around the time when she created the role of Soot in Durang's *The Marriage of Bette and Boo*. Olympia's body found the inner life of the character expressed in a gentle, constant, Parkinson nodding of the head in agreement to everything life threw at her. From the ground of this simple gesture grew an *effortless* performance. A fully embodied being subsumed Olympia's intentional framework. I once asked Olympia if she could have worked this way when she was younger. She told me that she didn't think she could have, because it took her years to refrain from levying excoriating judgments against herself or her characters. In the face of this greater compassion soot emerged.

At twenty-three, Tara accomplished this same feat by allowing the dream to have its influence. She worked effortlessly from a variety of incontrovertible needs, some of which escaped her awareness completely. Her performance resulted from, and gave shape to, a necessity that stretched the idea of "the objective." This Arkadina was a woman in extreme emotional circumstances behaving at the mercy of a chaotic mixture of unconscious motivations—much as she would in life. We could retrospectively interpret this behavior (and therefore arrive at the throughline of the scene), but that's an academic matter. In the moment of witnessing the scene, we were stunned by the immediately recognizable human situation that was taking place before our eyes.

I don't doubt that characters have basic throughlines. But I find it reductive to say, "This one thing, barring obstacles, is what this character is driving toward from the beginning of the play to the end." Realistic psychological plays are primarily constructed of cause and effect, yet great performances manage to transcend it and still render the throughline of the character. I teach reciprocal action, objectives, and obstacles, and I stand by their clarity and their agency as a *via positiva*. But in these latter days I feel the need to inject theater with more of the chaos of life; the conflicting drives that have equal pull, until one valance loses some of its potency. I want more life on the stage. We act from such a variety of necessities and drives that we cannot even tell what we're about half the time. We think we are moving in one direction and a phone call comes and pulls us, perhaps only momentarily or perhaps irrevocably, in another. I am not suggesting that the theater be life, but only that acting could be more lifelike by permitting greater, nonlinear (yet recognizable) chaos. What would happen if the unconscious of the character, that which is not known to her yet, is at play at the same time as her conscious intent? If our unconscious minds are years ahead of our conscious desire, could that not find its place onto the stage as it does in our behavior in life? What seems like chaos in that instance might not be chaos at all, but a purposeful working out of life.

What emerged in Tara's scene was the unconscious mind and behavior of the character. But I was struck by the irony that we had to return to the traditional route of rehearsing and making use of objectives and action in order to arrive at that point. So, no wholly organic model of acting was in the cards.

On the heels of this experience came another of equal value. Manish and Linda were playing Trigorin and Nina in their lengthy seduction scene in act 2. During rehearsal the scene developed nicely. Manish's work in particular surprised us with its langour. Chekhov parallels this scene with the presentation of Treplev's earnest, symbolic drama in act 1. Manish and Linda's scene looked like a satyr play by contrast. There was only one problem: Linda was having difficulty with her opening soliloquy. She disrespected Nina's starry-eyed craving for celebrity and celebrities. Linda judged it harshly, and she was consequently frustrated by her inability to imagine her way into those few lines preceding Trigorin's entrance. Robert worked up a two-minute incubation: Linda experienced the sensations that followed from Nina being stifled at her father's home, and then the sensations resulting from her freedom on Sorin's estate across the lake. She then held both of these states together simultaneously. Embodying the tensions between these polar states and then holding them together created the seed that grew into Nina's pressing need to escape. This was the incubation image she was to re-experience before going to sleep.

The week after creating her incubation image, Linda burst into the rehearsal room and in an extremely uncharacteristic fashion insisted that we work on a dream she'd had a few days earlier. I don't recall who was in the rehearsal room at the time, but I do know that Manish had not yet arrived. The quote I include here is a condensed version of the landscape Linda found herself in while re-inhabiting her dream.

> I am in a large open courtyard with lots of lush, green grass . . . I'm barefoot and wearing a white, loose, flowing dress. It's very early morning and the sky is hazy . . . Morning dew is on the grass and I'm running around, happy, feeling clear and alive. My skin feels fresh and clean and dewy. I feel a cool breeze. It's a little damp . . . As I walk, I sense that someone is behind me. I do not turn around but speed up instead. Suddenly, someone grabs me from behind and twirls me around. I turn and see Manish and feel instantly relieved that it's him. He has a very strange look in his eyes and I try to smile but it vanishes as he backs me up against the wall of the bathhouse. I feel frightened but a little excited as my back hits the wall—it's a very cold, smooth marble wall. My face is hot but my body is cold from the wall. He stares at me intently and then starts to kiss the perspiration on my neck and chest. It's very slow and deliberate and soft. I don't know how to respond. I don't touch him, but feel my resistance and fear melting away as I close my eyes and begin to enjoy his touch.

Robert crystallized these points: the dewy feeling of her skin, the cold marble on her back, and the hot, excited, sweaty feel of her chest and face.

Manish arrived, unaware of Linda's dream, but more importantly, not a witness to Linda's dreamwork . Linda and Manish went directly into the scene. Gone was the playful, adorable Nina and gone was the weary satyr practicing his ancient line on an innocent youth.

This virgin was ready to give as good as she got. What we watched was a young woman on the brink of her first sexual experience. She didn't know how to initiate this encounter but she was ready for it. She was neither lewd nor bawdy. She was simply ready. Nina's ambition—which had presented such problems to Linda—was at play. Seen through her eyes, Trigorin was to be her initiator into three great mysteries: art, love, and sex. Nina had awaited this moment with simultaneous eagerness and calm. Her vital expectant presence filled the stage. It was no wonder Trigorin wanted to possess this girl of such potential! How much purity, seriousness, and passion she had to offer![2]

But a new problem arose. The fresh novelty of Linda's performance derailed Manish's. In rehearsal Manish had let himself indulge in the sensuous enjoyment of Trigorin's sexual mastery. He seduced Nina with dissolute tales of his moral and aesthetic weakness, focusing intently on his own enjoyment and stimulation in the process. In response, she had lapped him up in all innocence—to his even greater delight. I had been satisfied with the direction the scene was taking: Trigorin-as-narcissist, seducing Nina as he seduced himself. But after re-evoking the presence of Linda's incubated dream (in which Manish figured prominently) Nina was transformed. No fawning child, she yearned for the skillful touch of an experienced man. She needed to be swept up, lost in him, ravaged. No gropings, no sighs, no youthful diffidence would do. In other words: no Treplev. She needed more than Trigorin's narcissistic self-stimulation. She needed him to focus his mastery and assurance on her. The difficulty was that in the face of this composed, sexually ready Nina, Manish actually

---

2. This change in Nina obviated the objections to her character that I had made weeks earlier. Linda's performance made me feel sympathetic to Nina's desires and ambitions.

turned into Treplev, a young man in his early twenties who certainly wasn't without charm, but was simply too unsophisticated to deliver the goods.

We didn't get much further in this scene. When Manish did experience the full force of his sexuality as an actor it was by surrendering to the workings of his imagination as expressed in a dream.

CHAPTER SIX

Dream
Homeopathy

A few months later, Manish, Tara, and I decided to incubate dreams on another play, *Much Ado About Nothing*. They had just finished playing Beatrice and Benedick in a very good production directed by Michael Ouellette. Manish's performance had been wonderful. He was clever, charming, and skillful with the verse. He was particularly good in the scenes with the men, warmly embracing the intricacies of Benedick's relationships with Claudio and Don Pedro. Tara's performance was good, but she felt she had not fully realized her potential. Her relationship with Benedick had been spontaneous, familiar, and affectionate, but there was little emotional or sexual heat between them—and this seemed an essential ingredient to me. The same old problem—sex—had reared its ugly head on both sides, Tara's and Manish's. When the play closed, I asked if they'd like to incubate dreams on Benedick's and Beatrice's first encounter.[1] They agreed.

---

1. *Much Ado About Nothing*, act I, scene I.

When we met in my office, I asked them to talk through the scene with an eye to the point at which they felt most engaged. I knew that a powerful state of attraction exists between Benedick and Beatrice and that it must be inherent in every word Shakespeare wrote for them. This sexual state had been potentiated for the two actors but had somehow failed to crossed the boundary from character to performer. The moments when the actors felt most engaged had to be those in which the attraction was most present.

Manish located his moment easily. "What, my dear Lady Disdain! Are you yet living?" Manish entered the moment in his present imagination, not in his recollection of the staged scene. Everyone's attention suddenly focuses on him as he addresses Beatrice. It scares him. His eyes feel cocky. His smile feels nervous. As he speaks his energy leaks out of his midsection. He shifts his weight back to his left foot, and the leaked energy surrounds him. He takes a breath to draw the energy back into his body as he completes his second line. He points a finger at Beatrice in order to direct the full force of his newly gathered energy at her.

His incubation image was the feel of his cocky eyes belied by his nervous smile, the energy leaking out from his midsection as he shifted his weight back to his foot, and his energy drawn back into his body only to be released at Beatrice as he points his finger at her.

When it was Tara's turn to tell her most vivid moment, she flashed me a despairing look as if to say, "There ain't one moment when I'm engaged." I asked them to go through the scene again. This time I paid close attention to Tara's body for flickers of involvement. During the second reading, I noticed two moments when Tara's body came alive. The first was when Benedick says his outrageous, "God keep your ladyship still in that mind! so some gentlemen or other shall 'scape a predestinate scratch'd face!" and the second was when she spoke her own last line, "You always end with a jade's trick. I know you of old."

Tara's reaction to Benedick's line was clear: It was one of scandalized pleasure. She reacted with a throaty laugh, a twist of her thrown-back shoulders, and a piercing look. Her reaction to her own line was deflation. These physical responses contained enough contrast to prepare an incubation image, but frankly I would have used any two images that arose that even whispered of belonging to different states.

In working up the incubation image with her, I presented the lines sequentially. But Tara unconsciously reversed the order—responding first to the last line, "You always end with a jade's trick. I know you of old." She enters the landscape at that line and discovers tension in her throat and back. Her breath is blocked. She patiently attends the tension and enters it. When she does she finds herself standing on a dark road in the woods. An abandoned car is parked in front of her. It is the inhibitor of her breath. We then move to Benedick's first line. His outlandishness releases her breath and makes her feels like a child filed with boundless energy. Her body comes alive and she feels as if she has to jump. I honored Tara's sequencing of the images and prepared the incubation. She was to experience the tension in her back and throat; the car on the road in the woods, blocking her breath; and the boundless, jumping energy coursing through her body in response to Benedick's quip.

The following week Manish, Tara, Robert, and I met in a rehearsal room to work on the dreams and apply them to the acting. Tara had only one dream to report, but it was a beauty:

I am in the Gap by a table in the back near the dressing rooms. Women dressed in the familiar Gap employee outfits—khaki pants and white tees—ask my opinion of the clothes. I am amused. Our interaction is extremely superficial. The light is fluorescent. Then the dream changes scene and I am at a club where a film festival is about to begin. I am to meet Manish and Mac [the actor who played Don

Pedro]. The lighting inside is dark with a royal-purple tint. I am
eager to go inside and meet them. I pay $3 at the door.[2]

As Robert and Tara worked to re-enter the dream landscape, she
experienced the sensation of light around her clothing as "surface-y,"
as though a breeze were passing over the hairs on her arms. When
Robert asked her to go *beneath* that light she found an abysmal darkness between her skin and clothing. The quality of the air there was
"very heavy, depressed" and she experienced a silent loneliness.
Toward the end of the exploration, Tara experienced the "eager feeling" in her legs while she was paying the $3 entrance fee to join
Manish and Mac in the club. We couldn't help noticing that this
actor, who had held back from entering fully into the play, was now
eager to pay the entrance fee. That had to be a good sign.

I was impressed by the creativity of the autonomous imagination.
Beatrice's final line in the scene, "You always end with a jade's trick. I
know you of old," evoked a B-movie image of loneliness, a dark road,
and a lone car that inhibited her breath. The dream transubstantiated
this into a more abstract image, but one that was composed of Tara's
deepest autonomous imaginings: the contrast between the amused,
"surface-y" light on top of her clothes and the depressed, abysmal
darkness between her clothes and skin. It reminded me how important
it is to respect whatever imaginative objects arise when doing both steps
of the process. Honor what comes up and imagination will rebound
with richer material. While developing an incubation image, if an actor
begins to describe the location of "Get thee to a nunnery" as happening on the set of Kenneth Branagh's *Hamlet*, so be it. Trust the actor's
imagination to work its way through to deeper content in dreams.

---

2. Note the passageway into a better world. This is a familiar dream theme,
   and one that we have had significant success exploring. We do so frequently
   in later dreamworking.

Manish's dream was really funny and perfect.

I am with my ex-girlfriend at a club watching a taping of *Dallas*. She
scornfully tells me, "I don't think those people you look up to are
going to help you succeed as an actor." I flash her a nasty look and
wonder, "Why are you always like this? You don't even know them."
On the dance floor in front of us, J.R. and a wildly sexual SueEllen
(of *Dallas* fame) are acting a steamy love scene. SueEllen is in bed
watching the approaching J.R. with scorn. Their faces meet. Her
body is sweaty. Then the dream shifts to a heavy, metal exit door. I
run to Larry Hagman to compliment him on the show. Hagman is
extremely tall with very broad shoulders and a wrinkled, tense face. I
feel tiny in comparison. With childlike joy and nervousness I say,
"Good show, Mr. Hagman." Larry Hagman asks me if I've told that
to the producers. When I say I haven't, Hagman is annoyed and says,
"Then what's the point?" and walks out the door.

While exploring the dream, Manish first inhabited the scornful
look on his ex-girlfriend's face. He then transited into Larry Hagman
and felt how Hagman looked upon him as an annoying boy, a
"nonentity" (shades of Treplev in *The Seagull*). Hagman, on the other
hand, was brimming with sexual confidence and manly arrogance.
Manish experienced Hagman's broad shoulders and manly arrogance
and how they were contrasted by a physical imbalance he felt as he
inhabited Hagman's body. He then effortlessly re-experienced the
marked contrast between the broadness and the dream-Manish's delicacy. At one point in the process Manish also identified with and
entered into SueEllen's body without any prompting.

After Robert brought the exploratory dreamwork to an end, I
asked the two actors to try the scene again. During this run-through
Larry Hagman was there with Manish in his body. Manish wasn't
pretending a masculine sexuality; he embodied it. Moreover, when he

glanced at Tara, he spontaneously projected into her elements of the wildly lusty SueEllen. These materialized immediately in Tara's receptive body and freed her acting. There are all sorts of psychological terms for this phenomena; psychoanalysts call it projective identification, Jung called it a kind of psychic infection, and the gestaltists say that it indicates confluence at the contact boundary. But to me it simply seemed like a raw connection between people in direct relationship. In the performances they'd given during the original *Much Ado* run, Tara had been a "shadow actor"[3] to Manish, lending him her energy and depleting her own. The contact between them was assured, but it was soft. Now, facing a sexually robust, challenging partner, Tara took up the gauntlet and the scene caught fire.

The playfulness, eagerness, and excitation between them continued until Beatrice's "You always end with a jade's trick. I know you of old." Tara had understood the line intellectually, but couldn't fully find it emotionally. Had no man ever given her the coup de grâce and then split while the going was good? No. This time through, Tara touched on the dark, depressed feeling of her skin. As Benedick departed, her body sagged and she stood haunted, stung and alone. The question of whether she understood the line emotionally was moot.

And I now understood why she had transposed the two lines when we prepared the incubation image. Tara intuited that the play opens with Beatrice's fear that what happened once between Benedick and her might happen again. If she risked loving him again she would once again find him her equal in wit, passion, and intellect—and then he'd abandon her again for the company and safety of men. She would be left alone. Again. In the absence of Benedick's proven emotional commitment, all of their amusing repartee was simply a "sur-

---

3. Janet Sonenberg, *The Actor Speaks* (New York: Crown, 1996), 249.

face-y" light, beneath which lay a terrible sadness for Beatrice—and for Tara.

An addendum: In later days Manish told me that Larry Hagman came unbidden to the rescue in whatever play he was currently rehearsing. When Manish didn't know what to do, Larry injected his work with confidence and decisiveness.

CHAPTER SEVEN

A Machine and
a Miracle

I was to direct my students in Corneille's play *The Illusion*, adapted by
Tony Kushner. Robert and I planned on incubating dreams with the
cast. *The Illusion* is set in the cave of the magician Alcandre, who is
served by the Amanuensis. Pridamant, the punctilious bourgeois
lawyer, comes as a pilgrim seeking Alcandre's services. Pridamant's
tempestuous relationship with his son ended in a rift fifteen years earlier, and he longs for a reconciliation before he dies. Unable to locate
his son, he comes to Alcandre's cave hoping for a miracle.

Alcandre produces a series of three visitations for Pridamant—
guaranteed to be real—in which the son's life is revealed. Each visitation contains a male lover (the son) a female lover, a maid, and a rival.
Each successive visitation shows the quartet of characters in increas-
ingly advanced stages of age, experience, wisdom, and pain. Oddly,
their names and circumstances change with each visitation although
their histories advance. In their carefree initial encounter they are pas-
sionate, heedless youths. In the third, which seems to take place years
later, the lovers are miserably married, and the son's infidelities are

desperately dangerous. Only risky conquests make him feel alive, and he conducts an affair with his patron Prince's wife. Locked in a ghastly marital confrontation the son and his wife confess the truth: their lives and deaths are inextricably bound by their love for one another. In this small, hopeful moment, the betrayed Prince arrives. He stabs the son in the heart. Tied to him in life and in death, the wife also perishes.

Bereft, Pridamant's heart breaks at their deaths. But then . . . Alcandre reveals that they are not dead at all! These were just scenes from plays these actors had performed. His son is indeed alive, a member of this promising acting company in Paris, twelve shows a week, and if Pridamant wishes he can make Paris by dawn. An actor? The theater is really such an indelicate profession, so unseemly. Banished are Pridamant's thoughts of reuniting with his son. He leaves the cave with his heart intact, unable even to recall his actor-son's name. Alcandre, disheartened, his magic having failed to alter the human heart, leaves the Amanuensis to close up shop. As he sweeps, the most theatrical of the play's characters, Matamore the lunatic (a fifth character whose heart is scarred by the lovers in the second visitation), crosses the boundary from the play-within-the-play into the real world of the cave. The lunatic seeks the perfect solitude of the moon where he can never be hurt again. The Amanuensis directs him on his way to the shining, glorious orb, and the play ends.

On first reading *The Illusion* a year or so before it was time to really think about it as a director, I delighted in the synthesis of Corneille's witty plotting with Kushner's psychologically perceptive New York humor. It made me laugh. The play seemed to be a pretty bagatelle, with a bitter theater-insider's joke at the end: the bereaved father could reunite with his son but rejects him because he is an actor. When I re-read it after many months, in preparation for working on the play, I was astonished to find it depressing. For all its genuine humor, this is a dark and melancholy play about the consequences we face as a result of our ungoverned, and even our governed, natures. Characters initially depicted as mechanical devices transform into individuals who sow their own unhappiness and demise. Those who manage to escape their natures do so at the cost of emotion. Those who retain emotional lives do so at the cost of pain. This play shows human beings as failures. Moreover, theater itself is portrayed as a failure. The Amanuensis is ravaged by the despicable roles Alcandre forces him to play. The magician effects a change in his audience that lasts only for the duration of the performance. By the time Pridamant leaves the cave his broken heart reforms and its dry crumbs reassemble. Worse yet, he is better for having had his catharsis and can return complacently to his life now that he has shed those pesky emotions. *The Illusion* presents theater's only enduring success as the creation of characters who cross the boundary of the play and live on in the audience's minds. (I think about Hamlet almost every day. He might as well be a member of my family.)

So much for first readings. My delightful little bagatelle had turned into a pessimistic and penetrating look at love and theater. It was cutting a lot closer to the bone—mine—than I liked in this situation. I prefer working with my students on less personally troubling material. The students' excitement committed me to the project. I was not happy, but I had to find my directorial way. So I turned my attention to the frame of the play, the relationship between Alcandre and the Amanuensis, and the illusions they produce for Pridamant. In order to envision the nature of the magic in *The Illusion* I'd have to comprehend the history and complexities of the magician's and his assistant's relationship and what brought them to this cave. I'll spare you most of the details, except to say that after a fairly arduous search of the play and myself, I came to realize that the nature of the magic had to be the magic of theater, no hocus pocus, no engineered illusions.

That decision made in a general way, I still found myself troubled by a single action of Alcandre's that I could not understand. It occurs in the second set of vignettes. Pridamant threatens to leave the cave if Alcandre doesn't alter his son's fate right there on the spot. Alcandre complies, according to a stage direction, with a "motion in the air, and Lyse (the maid) is struck by a change of heart," thereby saving his son's life. Although I understood the magician's need to keep his audience, I couldn't feel my way into the system that must exist between Alcandre and Lyse in that moment. When I complained about this to Robert one day he sweetly inquired, "Do you think, Janet, that you may have overidentified with Alcandre?" In my effort to contend with the personally challenging issues posed by *The Illusion* and in figuring out the way the play works, I kept seeing the piece through the eyes of the magician-auteur. This is a sorry state for a director who must tell all the characters' stories, not just one. I—as Alcandre—was at the center of the action, and I had to get out of my own way. "Um, yes."

Robert suggested I do the dreamwork. He begins preparing my incubation image with, "What do you see?" I reply,

> Lyse is standing in the darkened garden. The moon is rising and falling without any rhyme or reason, threatening. She has just sworn deadly revenge on her lover with a sweep of her arm—it is final. Pridamant, watching her, insists that he cannot tolerate witnessing his son's demise "in this sea of sharks." Alcandre, realizing his client is about to leave, panics [the ultimate power of the audience, leaving the theater; I experience this intensely as I watch the scene in my mind's eye], motions in the air, and Lyse is struck by a sudden change of heart, saying, "On the other hand. . . ."

I see that it is all hands, Alcandre's panicked waving and Lyse's avenging arm-turning into . . . "On the other hand."

Robert asks me how Alcandre feels.

He is about to lose his audience.

I see myself sitting in a rehearsal room, reaching deeply with an imaginary hand into an actor's body, trying to find the link that will connect him to my vision and that will keep me "from losing my audience," in this case, the actor. This feeling is familiar to me, and my body is flooded with sensation. In my mind's eye I see my hand extend magically into him to pluck the inspiration that will create the connection. I experience a feeling common to me, an embodied sense that life is expressed all in the hands. As my left hand extends to reach deeply into the actor's mind, searching for images, my right hand covers my cold nose. My eyes look deeply within. The physical and emotional feelings are fully embodied, and set in my being.

Robert then directs me to move to Lyse, the maid. I am distressed about having to go there, but relax and orient myself.

> What is it like to be betrayed and want revenge? What happens in your body?
>
> My left hand holds a man back with power, my solar plexus knots, my eyebrows arch, my nostrils flare. My right hand is held aloft.
>
> What happens on the line, "On the other hand?"
>
> I see the beach one summer, when my sister-in-law, Shelley, and I decided that "whatever" would be our new modus operandi in coping with life's exigencies. I tried it for months, but it led to a terrible dead-end experience, momentarily comforting, but ultimately the death of emotion. (Which parenthetically is precisely what happens to Lyse in the last third of the play.)
>
> My solar plexus relaxes, drawing down, my shoulders go with it, my faces breaks into a forced, tense grin of "whatever . . ."

As you can see, my imagination returned twice to real-life memories of its own accord, yet they joined themselves seamlessly to the
characters' experiences. This is common to the technique, and
remains a private experience for the artist. The dreamworker can easily work on these images without knowing their source.

Then Robert asks me to overlay the two images: the waving hand
of Alcandre with the "change of heart" text of Lyse. This is hard at
first. He leads me back through all of the physical sensations. I finally
do it with some ease and a new experience emerges. Master and the
puppet are lock and keyed in an immobile embrace. His waving left
hand, leading to her solar plexus that is forced to relax into the grin.
It was painful. The characters' interactions are inextricably bound. If
he is the puppet master he is just as locked into the experience as she.
Moreover, she doesn't have to like it! No human being enjoys emotional coercion, no matter how good for him or her. And what of the
actor who has constructed a role with one set of premises, has committed to them in performance, only to have them mutated into their
opposite by a playwright (or a director) who is pandering to his audience?[1] This revelation was made out of the sensation (of coercion in
the solar plexus that forced a tight grin) that I was given in the incubation image. The play has begun to direct itself.

From the point of view of the dreamwork, I was delighted to
realize that we could understand a system, the interrelationship
between two or more characters, by holding together each state and

---

1. Corneille railed against artistic coercion around the time he wrote *L'Illusion
   comique*. Chosen by Richelieu to be one of "his" five dramatists, Richelieu
   had ordered the playwright to write a particular plot device. Corneille did it,
   then rewrote it, and left for Rouen with the cardinal's wrath hot on his heels.
   Another possible motive for Alcandre leaving Paris with the Amanuensis?
   Phyllis Hartnoll, ed., *The Oxford Companion to the Theatre*, 4th ed. (London:
   Oxford University Press, 1983), 182.

seeing what emerged. In this case, by holding together Alcandre's embodied state and Lyse's embodied state, a third state came forth. It was there all of the time, inherent in the interaction, but by holding the two together and waiting, it emerged, fully blown. This became a crucial element of our later work, but it was early days yet for this kind of experimentation.

The physicalized question, the incubation image, posed to my sleeping imagination is contained within these images: the waving left hand, the solar plexus, and the forced, relaxed grin of "whatever." I repeat this for twenty seconds before I go to sleep—and the first night I had the following dream.

> My scientist friend comes down the stairs outside of my office building at MIT carrying an artifact that he brought back with him from an incubated dream. It is a large 30" × 30" square slide of surgical steel, perfectly machined, with hillocks of an oozy, black substance covering its surface. He is excited both for himself and for me. He has returned from the dream state with an actual artifact, a tangible answer to his incubation image! He wants to show me that the incubation process has worked. Before he can say a word I exclaim, "Oh my god, you've united my play with artificial intelligence!" Suddenly I realize that he is about to make a tragic experimental mistake. In my mind's eye I see him inserting the entire slide into a specially constructed disk drive. The artifact will be ruined, lost. With blinding "scientific" insight I realize that it must be done in layers.

No need to doubt that this dream was generated by the incubation image. I sensed its biting relevance the moment I awoke.

Robert and I work on the dream and he brings me first to sharp, pointed edges of the metal slide. He works slowly, having me observe the ooze and sense my reaction to it. "Heavy, dragging down." I am a little afraid of its immensity, and although it still provokes fear, I accustom myself to it by slowly and patiently remaining there. Robert then asks me to sense my way into the ooze. It is elemental! I am staggered by the fact that it's composed of a single element. What is its nature? Slow, moving at a remarkably slow rate, hundreds of thousands of years, millions, slowly. What is its nature? It is force. A wave of sensual intensity attends that force in my body. Robert asks me to overlay the force onto the characters of the play, which I do without hesitation. I sense that the force moves them without their awareness of its presence or power. They nevertheless are absolutely at its mercy.

The magician's and Amanuensis's creative urges, the drive to love, the sexual complexities inherent in the play, the rival's and the maid's jealousy, the son's predatory nature, the father's need to see his son, Matamore's and Adraste's love of Isabelle, are all driven by the same elemental force. It takes the form of love, sexuality, creativity, and their terrible analogs, jealousy, fear, and destruction. The force is infinitely malleable, but its dynamic, active presence is incontrovertible. That is *L'Illusion comique* and equally, the *l'illusion tragique.* What might we make of this titanic power if our natures could be aligned—if we were not our own predators and prey? What to do with this insight, now a physical reality for me? It was my responsibility to make certain that the actors' performances captured this driving essence, that they were hostages to it. And I saw quite forcefully that we would reveal all the machinery of the theater and then make the audience forget it. The magic we'd deal with was infinitely complex: the magic and mechanics of human relationships and the magic and mechanics of theater. This choice placed the entire burden of the creation of awe on the actors.

Rehearsals Begin

The Illusion was cast by auditions, using primarily student actors. I did not select actors with whom I knew the dreamwork had the maximum potential to work. My colleague, Michael Ouellette would play

the Amanuensis, the most difficult role in the play. I looked forward
to doing the dreamwork with him because he is an impeccable actor
with superb selectivity, and he is always game for an adventure in
technique. There were a few young actors whose depth of perception
was breathtaking and whose technique was fairly solid. There were
also some actors with little or no technique or training, but with natural talents. What would happen with the dreamwork in the hands of
inexperienced actors? What would happen with a company of actors
formed *ab ovo* in auditions, and not accustomed to working together?

The plan mirrored our earlier experience. We decided to use the
first several days to read and talk about the play, followed by two days
of preparing the incubation images. We would rehearse for a week,
and then meet for two sessions to process the dreams.[2] It was my
intention to launch the dream material as the need or opportunity
arose.

The first reading and the ensuing discussions were a bit daunting. Several of the actors did not know that acting was playing *with*
one another, so there were all too many encapsulated, static deliver-
ies, as opposed to meaningful, early connections. These militated
against listening, and otherwise adept actors were left stranded by
lesser trained scene partners. Significant discussions about the play
with the ensemble had not quite gelled, although a few actors were
off and running. I fully accepted that I served the double role of a
teacher and a director, and bringing the ensemble to the same level of
expertise was my responsibility, of course. But it was time to prepare
the incubation images, and I wondered, "Just what exactly will we be
incubating?"

---

2. Who knows how long we took to prepare each incubation! I seem to
   remember that both the incubations and the dreamworking were endless.
   Were we to do it today both steps of the process would take no longer than
   twenty minutes per actor.

Day five, and Robert arrived. Instinct told me that we should do one more reading of the play before we began incubating. I hoped against hope that something, *some* kind of contact among the actors, or between the actors and the text, would happen. It did. Actors who had *never* paid attention to anyone were doing so. They listened, they looked at one another, and they allowed themselves to be affected. They read fearlessly and mindfully, allowing the moments of love, attraction, melancholy, and menace to emerge for the first time. They were behaving like a company of good actors. They were transfigured, and I was astonished. The reason for this alteration suddenly struck me—they were preparing themselves to dream. They nervously recognized that they were about to open themselves up to a much wider field of experience. The actors, the play, and the wide sea of imagination all began residing in the same environment. They knew deep in their bones that they were committing themselves to conjoin the world of the play with their sleeping imaginations and that the product of such a union would be uncensored. As a group they committed themselves to a deeper process than they had ever experienced before. This reading took on echoes of that depth—it sidestepped present resistances and invited them to welcome contact.

Shakespeare wrote:

Weary with toil I haste me to my bed,
The dear repose for limbs with travel tired;
But then begins a journey in my head,
To work my mind, when body's work's expired.

Sonnet XXVII

It takes daring to set aside the peaceful release of sleep and choose to work in your dreams. A terrific silence fell over the group on this and the following night, as the incubation images were prepared. Nervous anticipation over becoming the subject blended with the awe the company felt as the question, "What do you see?" courted the actors' imaginations. Wonderful material began to unfold.

Not every actor's incubated dream produced a transformative acting experience. Indeed, there were only a handful of situations in which I felt that the actor's current level of internal structure and training could support the depth and nuance of the dreams. I describe here a few incubation images and incubated dreams, along with anecdotal accounts, from both the actors and from me. Each of these circumstances offered a distinct technical way of using either the incubation image or the dream itself.

Jeremy Butler: Pridamant

During the first rehearsal with Alcandre, Pridamant, and the Amanuensis, I brought up the issue of the violence of creating art, a central issue in these relationships. I inquired if any of the actors experience the pain of creation. Did theater exact its price? Certain that Michael, who played the Amanuensis (and is of an age with me) understood this subject all too well, I was stymied by the fact that the younger actors hardly knew what I was talking about. I barely recall the time when being an artist was not both pleasure and pain. Faced with two young actors who were blithe and bonny, I tabled the question.

Jeremy confronted many challenges as he prepared himself to play Pridamant. Pridamant is in his sixties and has had a recent heart attack—Jeremy is in his twenties and is robustly healthy; Pridamant is a father who, in a dyadic relationship, drove his son away—Jeremy is a son with a strong, positive sense of family feeling; Pridamant is a dry, cold lawyer with a frozen heart—Jeremy is a warm, engaged young man with a kind and generous heart. On the surface, the only quality they shared in common is discerning intelligence and an analytical bent. A summary of both Jeremy's incubation image and the transcript of the dreamwork follows:

The scene that I incubated was me seeing the tableau of my son stabbed by the Prince. My first physical feeling was that everything below my heart drops, all the blood, all the fluids in my body sink to the ground. Then I focused on the blood coming from my son's wound. I went into the Prince's body and the way he stands, and the tension and relish in his body as he holds the knife. I go into the feeling of his blood; how loud and hot it is. Then I move over into my son's body as the knife is jabbed through his heart, which generates a feeling as if neoprene rubber covers his body and his head and face. He wants to scream, but he can't.

Here follows Jeremy's initial telling of his dream, and the dreamwork process:

I live in a fraternity that used to be a warehouse, so consequently we have a lot of open space. There is a big staircase going up to the third floor. There is some kind of play going on. I have an image of electrical and gaffer tape and cables on the floor.

My best friend, John, has come across a flax bag. In it are some donuts—white powdered donuts. A couple of people start eating them. I don't think I do. At some point I realize that they come from John's father's tour of duty in Vietnam, and they are twenty-five years old. After I realize this I take a bite of the donut, perhaps just to say I had, and it is powdery and crumbles in my mouth. I don't even have the saliva to spit it out.

And then for some reason John has to kill has father and his brother. It's as if they have rabies or are lame horses, and John has to put them down. There are many people around and there is bustling movement. As soon as I realize that John must kill his father and brother, I turn around and everyone is gone. They disappeared because they couldn't deal with this. Even John's mother ran away.

I realize that I am not going to be able to deal with it either. I run up a couple of flights of stairs to get as far away from the event as possible—it is just about to happen—when I jump up out of a window and grab onto the ledge on the third floor. I am hanging there suspended. The wood is digging into my fingers. I realize that I am crying. My cheeks are cold and swollen with tears. Somehow I manage to pull myself up to the floor. There are some theater tech people on the first floor, and they have no connection to the event that just transpired.

Robert began.

You are in a big room? Then you go upstairs?

There is a spiral staircase and I manage to dart up two or three sets of stairs.

Do you see John at any point?

I don't think I can picture him.

Can you describe when the dream opens, the place where you are?

Off the commons is a dining room, and it is dark and the doors are closed. I have the feeling that that's where the play might be going on.

What is the feeling about the play going to happen?

I have the feeling that there are people watching the play behind the closed doors, but I don't feel any connection to the play.

And what is the first thing you can recall seeing?

The first thing I can recall seeing is biting into the donut.

Can you describe the donut?

It is a white, powdered donut. Very brittle.

Do you know at this moment that it is from the Vietnam era?

I do. And I bite into it sort of like jumping on a bandwagon, like I just have to do it. I feel that the donuts are related to why John has to kill his father and brother.

Go to the moment when you bite the donut and taste the feeling in your mouth. What is that like?

Dry, very old. Absolutely bland. Not a taste at all. I see crumbling particles. It is almost like biting into raw space. Or chalk. There is a light quality of air, and the particles are sucking down into my lungs—like breathing in confectioner's sugar.

Sense into that dry, powdery, old, air-like feeling. What is that like?

It is frustrating.

Can you feel the dryness and frustration?

Yes. It fills up my mouth.

Can you taste its oldness?

Yeah, yeah.

What is it like to taste this oldness?

Cold. Like a mummy's cloth.

Feel that old, old, old cloth, that taste.

Yes. It is strange but not altogether unpleasant. It feels white.

Now, can you see John anywhere?

I have a feeling he is to my right, but I can't picture him.

But you begin to get scared?

Yes, when I turn around and everyone is gone—that crystallizes how unbearable this is going to be.

Go to the place where you are hanging on by your fingers. Describe where you are.

There is a wood ledge. My hands hurt but it doesn't matter. Anything so I do not have to see the murder.

Can you feel yourself hanging on to the ledge so you do not have to see John kill his father?

Yes. It energizes my fingers so they have the strength to hold me up.

How does it feel in your body not to see the son kill the father?

My face is pressed up against the wall that has latex paint on it. It is comforting to have that sensation so I don't have to see it. The rest of my body feels completely exhausted from the emotional response to the realization.

What is the emotional sense in the body that the son is killing the father? When you realize that the son is killing the father?

It is like a scream. Every cell of my body screams at once.

Feel that scream.

Yes.

Now feel your cold, swollen, wet face pressed against the paint, how you don't want to see that, but every cell of your body is screaming.

Yes.

Stay with that. Now go to the old, dry, coldness of the powdered, crumbling substance.

Yes.

Stay with that for a moment.

Before we turn to the ways in which Jeremy used this chilling dream, I'd like to recount some of his observations on the process. First, when the whole group practiced recalling their dreams, prior to incubating images, Jeremy wrote in his journal,

> I had dream after dream last night. I kept making sure to wake myself up and write them down. By the end of the night there were scribbles all over the page by the bed, recording five or six dreams I'd had. However, when I woke up the page was blank. I had dreamt that I was dreaming . . . maybe I am obsessing over this?"

This concern is echoed days later after preparing the dream incubation, but in more specific and gravid terms.

> I did the dream incubation today, and if I am honest with myself, I am scared. . . . I was impressed by everyone's commitment to the process. After I observed it, I relaxed and prepared myself for mine by getting into an open state of mind. I felt free to go wherever I was taken, but I admit that everyone seemed equally free so either they prepared themselves in the same way, or this is something naturally inherent in the process itself. . . . I was ready for the visual stuff, but not for the physical component of the effects of what I was visualizing. It was intense. . . . If we have to keep visualizing it's going to be really tough. Tonight, when I switched back and forth between Franz [the son] and Ricky [the Prince] and went from relishing the Prince's power to the fear and terror of dying, it was real. If we have to repeatedly keep returning to these places over the next six weeks I don't know if I can take it. Sleep is the only way to escape, except now even that is gone. I am really excited about seeing what happens with this.

This is the only dream I had Jeremy incubate, so his fears were allayed, but his difficulties had only begun. The closer we got to performance, the more his fears were fulfilled. In the third week of rehearsal, I mentioned that Jeremy might want to "touch" on the dry, white chalky dust of the donut in his dream when he got to the final scene when his son dies. I gave no other direction. He recounted in his journal, "I'm confronting my son's death and my heart comes back together again. As I heal, I am no longer hurt, and I feel myself getting colder with every moment. My heart is not a warm, bloody organ. No, not at all; it is as dry as the donut's crumbs."

I preceded that moment with a brief improvisation in which Jeremy clutches his son's (imaginary) body to his breast. He wrote,

> Every time I clutch my son to me I am reminded of the Arthur Miller line about "the warm air bathing over me," and I feel as if the sun is hitting me and making my body glow. In rehearsal I was able to hold onto that for moments. Then my son transformed into a dead fish in my arms. There is no need to hold this dead fish of a son in my arms anymore. He serves no purpose. I am healed. I am really healed. My heart fuses back together again; I have achieved my goal. There is no obstacle and so love is forgotten.

This is a terrible realization, but true to the play.

> Confronting the falling, red curtain [that suddenly obliterates his son's death tableau] has become devastating. Even just sitting here writing and thinking about it scares me. . . . The dreamwork becomes clearer and more present each night. Maybe it is just listening to the Amanuensis's speech night after night, but hearing "dry white bone-like love," over and over again makes me re-inhabit my dream onstage in every performance. I don't know if I had a completely unconscious response to this speech before I incubated my image, but it is really amazing that this image, the image in my dream and my sense of my heart have such grounding in the text and in my performance. It gives

me chills just hearing Michael [the Amanuensis] describe something I
can visualize and sense so clearly. When I go to that place at the end
of the play, I remind myself of what my heart is made of and it
brings back the feeling of coldness in my bones.

I come back with both regret and pride to that first rehearsal
when I asked about the price of making art. Jeremy recounts the following during the hiatus between weeks of performance:

> I am scared shitless of (the next performance). The more I think
> about having to go back into that place . . . looking down the barrel
> of the show and thinking about that red curtain coming down on my
> dead son—it turns my stomach to knots and won't stop. The minute
> the last performance of last week was done I realized that I have to
> go right back into that place next week. . . . On the one hand it's a
> very real fear and on the other it is good that I connect so strongly
> with the moment that it affects me and lets the acting happen. Now I
> cannot help but connect to the Amanuensis in the moment when he
> crosses over the boundary from the cave into the other world. I know
> he is gong to have to jump into that body—my body—and live with
> the pain of the translation. It's damned scary. At our first rehearsal
> we talked about the "violence" of theater and Eddie [who played
> Alcandre] and I weren't quite sure what to say about it. I don't think
> that's quite true now.

Am I glad? Sure. Am I sad? Sure. We all know that a little bit of
knowledge is a dangerous thing, not only because it can create mis-
understandings, justifications, or abortive experimentation, but also
because a little bit of knowledge sparks the imagination, which
demands to be told stories that contain even more knowledge. More.
More truth, more whys, more hows. And that is a restless story.

Franz Elizando-Schmelkes:
The Son/Calisto/Clindor/Theogenes

When I came to MIT, Franz was a junior and already a sensitive actor. Even then he possessed onstage a quality that Arthur Roberts described as, "Acting from less ego than any other young actor—or just enough to get the job done." It was true: his acting had translucency. Now, years later, he returned to MIT to get a double masters degree, and somehow found time to do a demanding role in a play (with a demanding director). I knew that the combination of his talent, his inventive acting process, and our mutual faith in one another would create a salutary climate for the dreamwork.

Franz incubated the moment when Clindor, imprisoned, awakens from a nightmare about his imminent execution. He begins:

That's the moment that most troubles me.

Before the women come in? Give me the setting.

Tricky. I am in a cell but my nightmare is not in the cell I occupy. It takes place in a smaller cell.

Do you feel congested in the cell?

Yes, and I am fettered and can't move about too much. But I am not uncomfortably bound. There is a small window that casts a shadow. It's gray, medieval.

Is there action?

I am sitting and hear the footsteps of the guards.

What does it sound like?

It's not so much their footsteps, but the rustling of their clothes, swords, and metal keys.

What does it feel like to hear this?

Hopeless.

And where do you feel that?

It starts in my wrists and moves up to my stomach and to my shoulders

As you feel that, concentrate on the sounds of the keys and rustling.

I can't hear them anymore.

Notice that in incubating the image, and in the following processing of dreams, Franz loses his imaginative thrust. He readily recalls it, in part because it is anchored in his body in a sensate landscape, and in part because the dreamworker redirects his attention there, which springs his imagination.

Can you go to the sound?

They're just walking, not fast or slow.

Do they care or are they indifferent?

Indifferent.

Can you hear their indifference in their sounds?

Yes.

What does it feel like, their indifference?

It feels like they're from some other planet. I cannot talk to them. I desperately want to say something.

Where does it feel, this desperation?

In my sternum.

Can you sense how their life is on their planet?

Yes.

Can you describe what it is like to lead their lives?

They remind me of Falstaff; joyous, drinking, weapons around them, surrounded by friends.

How does it feel to be in that state?

Warm. Confusing. Dizziness. Things move too fast.

Can you feel the dizziness of things moving too fast?

Yes.

Where do you feel that?

My temples.

Stay with that feeling of things moving too fast and go back to your sternum and feel the desperation.

OK.

Franz locates and experiences that image and sensation.

At the same time feel the feeling in your sternum and the opposing feeling of dizziness in your temple. What happens when you hold these two opposing forces together?

My throat closes up.

What's happening in your throat?

My Adam's apple is dropping. I have trouble breathing. I get really dizzy.

Breathe.

It was not Franz's mild distress that brought this session to a close but the fact that we had reached a synthesis of the scene that would serve (we hoped) as a powerful seed to imagination. As Robert once said, "You need a strong call to penetrate the sleeper's dreams and get imagination's attention." The incubation image begins with Franz's feeling of hopeless desperation in his sternum that caused pain in his shoulders and stomach. Then he moves to the Falstaffian dizziness of the guards. Holding these two embodied images together simultaneously produces a "black hole" in his chest as if his sternum and back collapsed. His throat closes up, making breathing difficult.

In his journal entries that he kindly shared with me, Franz comments that, as with his experiences training and working with Yuyachkani (the Peruvian theater company), he found the technique of concentrating on physical sensation rather than emotion to be a powerful one. Emotion is acknowledged if it arises, but it is a part of the experience, not the central focus. The ultimate goal is one of imagination, where emotion is only one component.

Here is his dream.

I am with my graduate school friends. We typically hang out, go out, and do all sorts of stuff. We go into a karaoke bar and we see it's "Lesbian Night" there. We seem to be in the wrong place, but everybody wants to sing. So, of all people, Kurt, one of my best friends in the group, a very shy and introverted person who likes jazz, gets up and does this amazing choreography. He is dressed in a white and black suit. He sings "Big Spender," and plays the sax. He makes people relax and sing karaoke.

Robert begins to lead Franz back into the landscape of the dream.

Can you describe the members of the group and where you are when the dream opens?

The dream opens as we come into the bar. It has a rug, the walls, the seats—everything has carpeting. It's relatively tacky. The tables are black wood; they might be plastic.

The kind of light?

It's not dark. You can see across the room. It's kind of dim. There are colored lights.

And how do you feel in your body as you enter?

It's cold outside so I have my usual many layers of clothing. I just feel like my normal self, coming in and taking off my jacket and scarf.

Are the others doing the same? Are they ahead of you?

Yeah, they are ahead of me, but I am in the middle of the group. The dream starts when I go in, and others have already found a table.

What happens to you when you realize it's Lesbian Night?

I am amused by the fact that it's an issue for some of my friends.

Can you get a little into the atmosphere of Lesbian Night? What kind of atmosphere is it?

Well, in the dream it wasn't really anything special. I didn't even notice it; somebody else brought it up. It wasn't about the atmosphere, but about being in the atmosphere of my friends in that situation. That atmosphere was very annoying.

Can you feel the annoyance? What is it like in your body?

It makes my mouth dry. I have the impulse in my shoulders to slap someone.

Can you feel that impulse to aggression?

Yeah, but it's not like aggressive aggression. I don't want to beat anyone up. I just want to grab them and shake them. I can feel it in my
shoulders and collarbone.

Are there any specific people around you want to shake?

Yeah.

Can you focus on one such person?

Uh huh.

Can you feels what happens with this desire to shake? How does it
feel in the rest of your body to shake this person?

There is something constraining me.

Go into that which is constraining you. How does it feel in your
body to be constrained?

I am not sure if I can feel the constraint because the defense mechanism comes right on top of it.

Where is that defense mechanism?

In my face, my neck. I smile, kid around.

Now let yourself go back for a moment to the constraint and the
feeling that something is stopping you. Can you feel that

OK.

Look at the man who is about to sing. Can you describe what he is
like as he is about to sing?

He is shorter than most of the men there. He has this beautiful
smile. He is happy, proud. He is carrying his golden sax.

Can you feel how happy and proud he is in his body?

Yeah.

Can you feel in your body what it is like to be so happy and proud?
Can you describe what it is like to experience his body from within?

He stands perfectly straight. His wrists are relaxed. His face is relaxed.

Can you feel the song go through him?

Yes.

What is it like to have the song go through him with his golden sax?

Franz is silent but clearly engaged.

> If you can't describe it, just feel the song go through him and the beauty
> of his body as the song goes through him. Just note very carefully how
> you feel in your body. Now we are going to rotate. Go back to Franz
> and first feeling irritated, wanting to do something to this guy and feel-
> ing constrained. Go back into that feeling. Say when you're there.
> Describe what your body feels when it feels that constrained irritation.

> Like there is no space between the muscles of my stomach and my
> lower back.

> Feel that, note it carefully. Just stay with it, try to hold on to it, while
> we go back to the beautiful singer, his beautiful body and the song
> going through him with his golden sax. Try not to lose what you're
> feeling in your stomach. Do you have both? No space between the
> stomach and the back? The beautiful body, shoulders, spine, and the
> song going through him? Stay with that feeling.

Franz struggles with this, having some difficulty. Robert brings him
back to the incubation image.

Remember the feeling in your throat in the incubation image before
you went to sleep?

My whole throat has dropped down to my chest and I am really
dizzy.

Good. Now, feel the song go through that.

Franz has a demonstrable reaction and struggles emotionally and
physically.

What is happening?

Ay yay yay. I guess I want to cry.

All right. Go back to your friend on the stage. See his body. See the
beauty of his body, the smile, the song. Can you feel back into that?
What's happening?

Robert returns to an image that Franz finds both unthreatening and
pleasurable. It is a relief to go there.

It is like being dead already.

Say more.

It reminds me of heaven.

Franz's face breaks into an enormous smile. He would later write that
this experience of his friend, Kurt, was a physical ecstasy in which "I
exposed my throat and made my soul vulnerable to anyone around
me. My chest exploded my arms and fingertips away from my body
to receive this light of heaven."

The dreamwork took Franz between the dream and the incubation image. This is a movement we now recommend against. We no

longer move between incubation image and dreamwork, dreamwork and life, and so on. However returning to the image was expedient as a way to make the connection between the different states Franz entered in both. Since he had difficulty getting back to an image in the dream, Robert shifted to the incubation image closely connected to it and the work opened up further. Consequently, when Franz used the dreamwork, he drew from both sources. He explains that he prepared these images as the vertices of a triangle, such as we see in the figure, and would move through them each day with increasing fluency. It was comprised of three sites, each of which could be contacted via a visual image and specific physical sensations.

Angle "a" was the prison, with pain in the shoulder and stinging forearms. Angle "b" was the karaoke bar, with strained hands and fingers and constrained anger toward his friends. Angle "c" was Franz's friend Kurt dressed in white, playing his golden sax, attended by the physical sensations of his upper body shifting side to side and chin and spine reaching to the heavens. Moving between a–b–a effected the sensation of the black hole in his torso. It created the conflict necessary to Franz, the need to escape from hopelessness only to be thrust back into its depths.

Franz described the intense physicality of his experience with these images:

> The triangle could be traversed in any direction. Vertex 'a' was the
> prison scene. The desperation and the pain in my upper chest and
> shoulders as well as the stinging in my arms all came with it. I would
> then roll up side a–b of the triangle to vertex 'b' which was full of
> anger an anguish about my friends' behavior in the bar. I felt the stress
> in my forearms straining the muscles in my hands and fingers, and a
> ring, circling but not touching my waist, prohibited my movement.
>   Sliding back toward vertex 'a' I would start getting dizzy as I
> entered the world of the guards. My eyelids shut, my eyebrows raised,

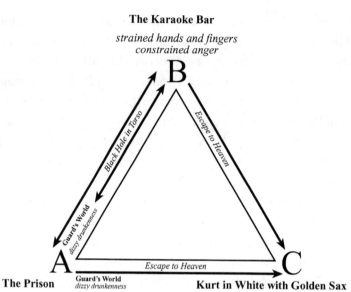

The Karaoke Bar

strained hands and fingers
constrained anger

The Prison

pain in shoulders
stinging forearms

Kurt in White with Golden Sax

shifting upper body
chin and spine reaching to the heavens

and the whole room began to spin. Then I slid all the way down to 'a.' Having been in the upper vertex made the pain of the desperation more intense and the stress of the anger and anguish more unbearable. The black hole between my lower back and my sternum began pulling me in gravitationally.

I traveled back and forth between these two vertices [a–b–a] and the drunkenness increased, making the space in my inner body smaller and the gravitational pull stronger. When throat began to close I escaped sideways to the vertex 'c' where my friend Kurt played his sax. It was beautiful, one of the most beautiful things I have ever imagined. It reminded me of being in heaven. Being there I truly could float and dance. My body was upright. An electric cord arced my back and neck so that I looked up to the heavens. I exposed my throat and my soul became vulnerable for anyone to see. My chest exploded my arms and fingertips away from my body to receive the light with my whole body. It was an ecstasy.

The return to the prison cell was unbearable. When I finally got there I experienced incredible desolation and a stronger feeling of hopelessness than before. I felt my body no longer existed and all that was left were my hands holding what used to be my body. Breathing was almost no longer necessary.

The image of the triangle was continuously on my mind as I worked.

Vertices and triangles—a very beautiful MIT image.

We applied the dreamwork to the scene from which the images were initially drawn, but not before working extensively in ways that Franz finds satisfying. I asked him to do an image theater exercise. He broke down four "nightmare images." I did not specify whether these were to stem from real dreams or from his imagination. He recounts them as (1) being trapped under the debris from an earthquake, for which he lay in an uncomfortable position between the legs of a chair; (2) reaching out his hand to try to save his brother from a disaster, in which his legs stood straight and he stretched out his upper body all the way to his fingertips; (3) on the verge of drowning and trying to burst up to the air only two inches above him, which had him on his back under the chair and reaching one hand up to the break the surface of the water; and (4) having his son "ripped from existence before his birth," in which Franz sat holding his knee as if it were his unborn child. Franz ran through these images, committing them to full, physicalized memory. Then he began working on the text, line by line, embodying one of the images and allowing it to give shape to the line. My premise in using this exercise was that since the soliloquy is a waking nightmare, then by using physical nightmare images we would immediately take it out of the reflexive physical world and catapult it into a more extreme and dangerous realm. Working slowly and intensely, this is exactly what happened.

Franz defined his next task. He had to take these nightmare images and shape them according to the movement of the text and the impulses of the character. In other words, he had to transform them into images for the play. This he did as "actor's homework," and here is when the dreamwork came into conscious play for the first time. Franz traversed the three vertices of the dreamwork triangle and blended them with the nightmare images.

> I moved up to the side to find the tension in my body and hands stem-
> ming from my anger at my friends. I incorporated that tension into the
> hopeless discomfort of the earthquake image, lay on my side, and
> began to speak. As I evoked my father in the monologue, I took the
> nightmare position of trying to save my brother, and I became empty
> inside, like a black hole. When I got to the "I am the child of fortune,"
> line I escaped into Kurt in his white coat, playing the golden sax.
> Leaving this heavenly feeling plummeted me back into the nightmare.

Franz worked in this way, developing an affective relationship among the character in a waking nightmare, the dream imagery, and the image theater exercise. Because the incubated dream images stemmed directly from the scene as "seen," they formed a natural bridge between the words and image theater exercise. It sounds like an elaborate process, and it is, although it reflects Franz's intense rehearsal methodology. His adaptation of the dreamwork was entirely his own, and I saw no need to interfere. Franz was on an intuitive jour-ney and after rehearsing in this way a few times, the words of the solil-oquy became "the words [he] would have said in that situation."

Franz used the dreamwork triangle as preparation each night. He did it in warm-ups and held it for thirty seconds before going onstage. If he used it any longer, it overpowered his body and once produced an unwelcome physiological response.[3] But when used discretely, he found

---

3. When his throat constricted and his sternum and back "collapsed," he actu-ally vomited.

that it allowed him to become vulnerable to the words and the situation, and, beyond that, it kept him vulnerable to his own imaginative workings. Franz commented, "I often describe acting as the art of standing inside-out onstage. You lose the skin that protects you from the outside, and walk onstage in a state of vulnerability. Perhaps the one thing we always hold protected inside our remaining shell is our dreams. The technique does away with that protection. You allow the audience to see through your body, into your dreams. This might be considered a sacrifice to make, but to the actor and to the audience it is a gift."

Michael Ouellette: The Amanuensis

In each of these anecdotal reports, the actors used the dreamwork in their own ways. In this final anecdote from Michael Ouellette, the dreamwork failed, but developing the incubation image succeeded.

The role of the Amanuensis is the most obscure, yet powerful, in the play. To what is he in service? To whom? It seems that he is in service to the whole play. That would encompass the magic, the theater, and the life of emotions. Is he that powerful? No, he is in service and often abased. But his power is such that nothing could happen without him. As a director, I humbly submit to the ultimate power of the actor. No matter how inspired a director's gifts, it is the actor who must embody the role, and it is the actor who experiences the pain and delight of embodying another being. The Amanuensis suffers powerfully. Alcandre says of him, "My visions are concocted through a violent synthesis. . . . [I]t costs, you see, it hurts, it's dragged unwillingly from the darkest pools. . . . I need his agony, I'm a chemist of emotions, his misery's my catalyst, it fuels my work."[4]

The role is subject to enormous interpretation. Largely silent, or silenced (literally made deaf and dumb by the magician), throughout

---

4. Pierre Corneille, *The Illusion*, trans. Tony Kushner (New York: TCG, 1994), 50.

the play, he has two scenes in which he speaks at length with titanic emotional intensity. The first is when Alcandre sends him into the play-within-the-play to enact Geronte, Isabelle's implacable, cold father. Hateful and vicious, does he love his daughter? Yes, "with a hard, cold bone-like love," but he loves her nevertheless. Every character in *The Illusion*, including Pridamant, loves; but their loves are framed, distorted or exalted, by their natures. The Amanuensis returns to the cave exhausted and spent, having paid the actor's price of embodying a character repulsive to him. There Pridamant, upon whose cold manner the performance was based, enthusiastically congratulates him. Here we have the first confrontation between the audience (Pridamant) and the artist (the Amanuensis) in which the artist realizes that his goal of touching the humanity of his auditor has failed. He sees a "fan," whose unthinking praise is arrogant and blind, a consumer's appreciation, not someone whose transformation he'd hoped to effect. Failing to make Pridamant reflect upon himself, the Amanuensis explodes in a wild, frustrated tirade on the stupidity of the audience and the fruitless anguish of the creative artist. He rails at Pridamant: "How I have to throw myself, again and again when he orders me to, into other lives, full of pain and twisted passion. . . .While baby-fat men like you sit watching, devouring like pigs the agony I produce."[5]

The actor playing the Amanuensis is faced with enormous challenges. He is the most direct link to the action and themes of the play: without him nothing happens, yet he must make these connections with full presence but without taking focus. Michael felt that his job as an actor was to make the connections between theater and love as explicit as possible. His incubation image gave him the visceral metaphor that created an interior landscape from which to work. He chose to incubate the moment when Alcandre incants the Amanuensis from the cave into the world of the play-within-the-play.

---

5. Ibid, 67.

> It was the moment of incantation when the magician sends me from
> the real world to the world of the theater where I have to embody the
> character, incorporating Pridamant. The physical sensation was of my
> heart enlarging to such an extent that it was pushing against my ribcage.
> It was if I had a bands of iron across my chest. There was an incredible
> tension, and pain, between the will of my heart to increase in size and
> the inability of my chest to expand and accommodate it. My knees
> buckled, and a cold shiver went up my arms. A scream of pain rose up
> from my chest, but is throttled off by the muscles in my throat.

Michael worked with this image throughout the play, but particularly in the actual scene in which the Amanuensis crosses over into
the play world. He commented,

> The resultant fused image of enlarging heart and constricting rib
> cage was there immediately, fully and completely and "real" for me
> physically. I didn't have to manufacture it. The physical manifestation
> was total. It was a physicalization of what I understand to be the
> basic problem of acting to be, at least for me, which is the desire to
> inhabit and project something bigger than my everyday self. . . . I
> don't see how I could have been more engaged physically or emotion-
> ally with the character's predicament than I was in the incubation
> exercise. . . . Geronte began to work because I allowed myself to
> inhabit the size of his pain and his anger.

I actually cannibalized Michael's throttled scream from the incubation image and used it in the play as a silent, frozen scream as
Alcandre rotates him on the turntable into the machine of the play.
We broke down the image in several ways and found a physical gesture that frightened both Michael and me.

Michael's dreams dovetailed precisely with early visions we had of
the character. But for a variety of reasons—not one of which was of

his doing—a definitive interpretation of the character's journey through the play took a long time to come. The dreams became less and less useful as the interpretation evolved, and we should have incubated another dream. But time pressed so we let things be. Michael did have one incubated dream that I believe found its way onto the stage for the audience to see, although he insists that he based this moment on an old acting teacher of his. He dreamt of:

> a beetle lying on its back on a strip of greenish-gray velvet. The beetle, though alive, looked like an artifact made out of highly polished beige marble veined with white. Its arms and legs thrashed frantically but mechanically to right itself. Suddenly it metamorphosed into a small, gnomish man of the same color, bearded and longhaired, like something drawn by Rackham in his illustrations for Wagner's *Ring*. The man was bent or squatting, flailing his arms, and screaming.

When the Amanuensis threw himself frantically at Pridamant in his maniacal tirade, he looked like nothing if not a mechanical beetle thrashing wildly, who suddenly recomposed into a disaffected fairy-tale gnome. This character resided in an imaginary landscape embodied in Michael, and I believe it emerged exactly as it did without his full intention. Or perhaps it was just as Michael said, and it was bound to emerge from this fine actor's being once he freed himself from the fear of looking foolish.

Reporting in all honesty I cannot say that using the dreamwork on *The Illusion* was an enormous success. Getting ready to dream catalyzed the most momentous event, the sea change in the actors' seriousness and attentiveness. A few actors had simply stunning—stunning—dreams that were spectacular outgrowths of the incubation images. I know that they served as superb, deepening research that brought them closer to the action and to the richly symbolic content of the play and their characters. Yet we did not always implement the dreams, and there was one occasion in which it just didn't work. Serving as both director and teacher was an enormous constraint for me. I was so busy just creating the play that bringing actors of wildly disparate levels of experience into the same universe felt like enough of a challenge. I didn't possess the inner space for reaching for the dreams with some of my students.[6] Or just as likely I just didn't quite know how to do it yet. It was early days.

I've detailed a few of the ways the actors themselves used the dreams and the incubation images. The co-opting of the process by the individual actors was heartening. But there was, indeed, one way in which the dreamwork pervaded the whole of *The Illusion*. When the work was really good, as it was on several nights, *it was my dream* that infused the whole. On the stage were actors who had nothing but the machine and magic of theater to create their illusions. Only a bench served as furniture. There were no more than five props in the piece, so there were few physical objects with which to create activity. When everyone's imaginations and concentration colluded on a given night, you could almost *see* the force on stage. No, I *could* see it on those nights. And, consciously or not, on those nights every actors' work was saturated with that force, and they worked exquisitely, in layers.

---

6. I now feel that if a director works with a group of actors all equally capable of bringing a high standard of performance into being, then implementing the dreamwork as a technique should be both easy and successful. Student actors, each at a very different level of expertise, posed insurmountable challenges for me as a director working alone. The dreamwork had its effects, certainly, but not the wholly transformative ones for which I was hoped. When we went to L.A. and worked with ten older actors, the transformation on the acting on all but one proved this point.

CHAPTER EIGHT

Virtual Reality

Alan Arkin and his son, Anthony Arkin, agreed to try the dreamwork process. They were in the midst of performing *Power Plays*, a series of three one act plays, at the Promenade Theater in Manhattan. Elaine May wrote two of the plays. The first featured May and her daughter, Jeannie Berlin. The last featured May and Berlin along with both Arkins. The second play was written by Alan and featured Alan and Anthony. Alan Arkin directed all three.

We planned to incubate dreams on the two-character play Anthony and Alan did together. We knew it would be an interesting endeavor for many reasons. Alan, one of the most imaginative actors in the United States, was making his reappearance on the stage after many years' absence. And Anthony is a talented, articulate actor and writer, whose vivid descriptive abilities would make working with him a pleasure.

The field of experience that we'd be incubating was very rich. As always, each actor and the play were part of the field, but in this instance we also had the complex relationships of a father and son acting together, amplified by the father having directed and written the play. The fact that they were already in the middle of performances was another aspect of the field. A sculpture of production had been created in which the performance, family, and interpersonal dynamics were built in. All these components created a complex world.

They each agreed to engage in the process for his own reason. Things that might enrich his acting or writing processes intrigue Anthony. Alan is specifically interested in the relationship between imagination and acting, and dreamwork certainly holds promise in that arena. Add to this that his work with his personal dreams in life is an ongoing one; by extension, using them in a new way held possibilities he was predisposed to appreciate.

Beyond this was another acting issue. When I'd interviewed him years earlier, Alan said that he no longer liked acting on the stage. The nightly repetition frustrated and bored him. When we spoke on the phone before doing the dreamwork, he wryly inquired whether this technique might smooth his resistance to simply getting on the stage each night. Since the moment in the play that most troubled or interested him seemed to find him offstage before the play's beginning, I suggested that he prepare for the first session in two ways. First, he should bring our traditional "what moment in the (scripted) play most interests or troubles you," and second, he should discuss his concern about getting onstage at the beginning of the session.

By the time we met, he decided to work on a scripted stage moment and let the other issue pass. I should have known that regardless of what we choose to incubate, pressing issues will always manifest themselves once the autonomous imagination presents itself. As you will see, it came into play as the end of the incubation session and framed Alan's experience.

Alan wrote *Virtual Reality* under unusual circumstances. He was learning the ins and outs of new scriptwriting software and, to facilitate this, had simply begun writing. He had written half the play before he even realized he was writing one.

Virtual Reality is set in an empty warehouse, where DeRecha (*derecha* means "right" in Spanish) waits for Lefty. DeRecha is middle management personnel fetishistically intent on following corporate directions to the letter. He does not care how much he knows, or how much information is withheld from him. He just does as he's told. Lefty, a fairly tough, young guy, has been hired to do an unspecified job that seems to involve some manual labor.

From the moment of Lefty's arrival, DeRecha makes irrational demands that perplex and trouble him; they make no common sense. DeRecha insists that they do a dry run—in pantomime—of their job, which is to unpack three crates soon to be delivered and check their contents against the waybill. Lefty agrees, but is confronted by the fact that DeRecha wants him to call off the items as they are "unpacked." Since Lefty has no idea what's in the imaginary crates this is a daunting and confusing prospect. DeRecha talks him into it, and so begins the journey in earnest in which Lefty's reality is deconstructed.

Lefty calls out the items as he "takes them out." At first he pretends what they are. Soon they begin to take on a pattern that frightens Lefty: a timer, guns, two Argentinean passports with their names and photographs on them, Himalayan survival gear, lanterns, and so on. When Lefty trips over one of the virtual lanterns the imaginary objects begin to make sounds that are audible to the characters and the audience. The pantomime becomes real to both men, and Lefty starts to panic over the implications of the "contents" in the crates. Just what kind of job is this?

DeRecha tells him to read aloud the "tent instructions" so they can assemble it. Lefty holds the imaginary instructions in his hand, and begins to read while DeRecha does the work of setting up the tent. The temperature drops and a cold (audible) wind blows through the warehouse. They start freezing in the "high altitudes of the Himalayas." DeRecha accuses Lefty of causing this catastrophe because he didn't pull any parkas out of the crates. When Lefty objects, DeRecha tells him that he was "the crate man" and had defined the entire contents of the waybill. A true statement in a virtual reality.

A sound of voices is heard offstage. By this point both men are in the grip of compelling unreality. DeRecha tells Lefty that "They," unspecified killers, are coming. DeRecha takes one the "guns" and goes to kill DeRecha, planning to shoot himself afterward. Lefty fights back, taking one of the "bungie cords," and strangles DeRecha. A terrific scuffle ensues in which both men are "killed," lying "dead" on the floor.

The noises offstage are the sounds of the real crates arriving. The virtual reality burns off like the morning mist. DeRecha turns to a stunned Lefty and says, "Nicely done old man, you did beautifully! Very nicely done. Things are going to work out just fine. Do you suppose you could give me a hand with these?"

In preparing any incubation image there are two main challenges: to lead the actor gently away from intellectualizing the imagery that reveals itself and to work slowly, allowing the images to become embodied. But we faced another challenge. Doing eight performances a week of the play had given the Arkins a visual and actually physicalized sense of their experience. This performance text had to be honored, but it could not be allowed to be more real than the imaginative artifacts that might spring forth while preparing the incubation images. This was compounded by the fact that the objects the actors handled onstage were entirely imaginary. Anthony and Alan had ardently endowed these imaginary objects with reality in both rehearsals and performances. Working away from what they experienced nightly might be trickier than working with actors who were in the early stages of rehearsal. The analogy between the dreamwork and unpacking virtual items from virtual crates is a good one: You never know what the autonomous imagination will body forth and then, there it is.

We prepared Alan's incubation image first.

Robert began,

Maybe you can describe the setting?

DeRecha deconstructs Lefty's reality beginning with imaginary objects until they become real. The moments that are difficult for me are those where the unreality has gotten so extended that we are actually constructing a tent onstage—an imaginary tent. We start to hear the sounds of the tent being constructed and the wind blowing. It's the construction of the tent that is not as rich as I think it could be.

With what kind of intention do you deconstruct Lefty's character?

My character's intention is basically to be a very obedient middle manager. I am under orders, and I want to do it right. I just happen to be insane and I pull him into my . . .

Are you standing or sitting?

I am active, building a tent. On my knees most of the time.

Are you talking?

I am mostly listening. Anthony is reading the instructions from a manual that doesn't exist.

Are you amused in any way?

No.

What do you feel in your knees?

I feel the pain of being on the hard wooden floor night after night and it is starting to be difficult for me.

And what do you feel in your back?

I feel nothing in my back. Even in life I almost never notice the tension I feel in my back.

Are you moving your hands?

Yes.

And you're hammering with your hands with an imaginary hammer?

No I am bending bars, lifting cloths, zipping and unzipping things, bending and unbending the poles.

Can you feel the cloth of the imaginary tent?

Yes.

What does it feel like?

It's interesting, because it's not what it's supposed to be. It's sailcloth and it should be rip-stop nylon.

New information has been delivered by the autonomous imagination. This moment requires nurturing. But because it is surprising, Alan shifts away from the experience to observe it. Critical observation can easily cause an actor to exit autonomous territory. Robert redirects Alan's attention to sensation and back into his body in the imaginary landscape.

Stay with what it is. It's as Janet said before, we might now be moving into the reality you feel rather than the onstage reality. So, is the cloth rough?

Yes.

And do you have it folded in your hand, or is it flat in your hand?

It changes as the section of the play goes on. At first it's completely rolled up and then I flatten it down.

Alan's tone of voice is factual. It has lost the thoughtful, evocative shading it had moments ago when he described the fabric as sailcloth. It feels to me like he is in the historic reality of performance. Robert brings Alan back to the present imagery.

Let's slow this down. How thick a roll is it at first?'

It's the size of a comforter if you had it bundled up.

Are you holding it in both hands?

Yes.

And as you begin to unfurl it, are you using a lot of effort?

No.

And does the weight change?

From this point on there is a shift. Alan's breathing deepens, his head thrusts back. He becomes more and more identified with what he sees in the present in his imaginary landscape.

Yes.

And can you feel it change?

Yes, as I unroll it on the ground it becomes lighter until there is almost no sense of weight.

Are there any smells?

The smell of sailcloth and hemp.

How does it make you feel, the smell of sailcloth?

Lively. There is a great sense of life to it. Organic. Smells of the outdoors, the sea and the woods.

Does it give you a body sensation when you have the cloth in your
hands?

Yes, a sense of vitality.

And can you feel it in your skin?

Not particularly.

In your veins or your muscles?

My lungs. I feel the blood being invigorated, aerated, and purified by
it and its associations.

Now as you feel that, what does the voice of the other person who is
reading the manual sound like to you?

Technical and slightly off-putting. Off-putting because its technical-
ity is at odds with the invigorating activity.

And how does that off-putting influence your body?

Are you talking about now or onstage?

Now.

I feel rushed.

And what does that do to your hands?

It makes them a little awkward.

Can you feel the awkwardness of the hands?

Yes, and the cold.

Can you feel the cold hands and at the same time the invigorated
lungs?

Yes.

What is it like to have that tension between those two states of
being, the hands and the lungs?

In asking about the tension between the state of the hands and the
state of the lungs Robert was investigating whether there was an
opposition worth exploring. Had there been he would likely have
moved back and forth between them or held them together, waiting
for the latent state—that contained both in opposition—to emerge.
Alan reported otherwise.

> It is still good. The cold hands don't bother me. I feel like they are
> part of the process.

> Feel the cloth in your hands as the tent that begins to develop. Can
> you describe the texture of cloth again?

> It is sailcloth, canvas.

> Can you smell it again?

> Yes.

> Feel into the texture of the cloth. Feel that cloth all around you.
> What is it like to be in such a roll of cloth that is being made into
> the tent?

> Very secure. Amazingly strong.

> Can you feel in your body that strength of the material?

> Yes.

> How is that strength of material being unfurled in your body?

> I feel very unified, whole, permeable . . . and yet very solid at the
> same time.

Can you feel what it is like when the constructed tent is completed?

Very, very secure. A little home, a house, protected from the elements.

Can you feel that in your body, that sense of the secure, cloth home?

Yes.

What does it feel like to be in such a tentlike body?

If Robert had asked Alan to transit into the "tentlike" body too early, he might easily have become confused or annoyed ("What do you *mean*, 'What does it feel like to be in such a tentlike body?' That's not even a human language!") or might have answered in a detached, observed way. By this point, however, the sensations of the cloth are so embodied that Alan has entered into a deeper fusion that is more organic: self as cloth and cloth as self. He is no longer outside of the experience, but joined to it.

It feels wonderful. Safe, secure and still permeable. Air going in and out of the pores.

How is the breathing similar or different from the invigorated feeling in your lungs before?

The breathing is slower. More peaceful.

As you listen now to the voice of the man who is reading, what is that voice relating to you?

It is an annoyance. Pushing.

Is there an intention of pushing in the voice?

No.

What is the mood of the voice?

It is trying to please, to do good, to be correct, but it is still pushing me.

Can you sense what it is like to try to please like that?

From the inside of it? I think so.

Keep on listening to it and feel what it is like from the inside of the spoken voice. What kind of body comes from that sense of the spoken voice?

A lot of physical strength. Unaware of the extent of the strength.

Can you feel into that strong body that is unaware of the strength?

Yes. It feels good.

How is it different from the man on his knees?

It feels very integrated, very cohesive, of one piece. Younger, more agile. There is a purity there.

Can you let yourself feel that purity throughout and see what happens to you?

There is a kind of innocence.

Where in your body can you feel that innocence?

My head.

Stay with the feeling in your head for a moment. Now go back to the moment with the cloth when you feel your cold hands. Feel the lungs that are filled with the smell of the cloth, invigorated. Can you feel that?

Alan does so.

Can you sense back in the tent that it is a safe place, yet permeable, and the way that is in your lungs?

Yes.

Now try to feel all of these things together: the innocence in the head, the feeling in your knees, the coldness in your hands, these two different ways of feeling in your lungs, the smell of the cloth.

You want me to feel both characters simultaneously?

Yes. What is it like to feel all of that together?

It feels very big. It feels like I am expanding, like I am feeling everything in the theater.

OK. Stay with that. Can you describe the feeling?

Yes, slightly unrealized and anticipatory. Hopeful and warm and anticipatory—but slightly unrealized.

I sense that we are heading for unanticipated rapids. What an actor experiences while doing the incubation image is often unexpected, but this one worries me. By bringing together these images, is Alan uncovering his malaise regarding the stage? I believe so. Robert, unaware of Alan's stage-fatigue, begins wrapping up the process.

Now this feeling—do you know this feeling?

I know it—it is what I feel every night onstage at that point.

We will stop here. For the incubation feel the innocence of the head, the coldness of the hand, the smell of the cloth and how invigorating it is. Feel the tent that is permeable and strong, and then this feeling that comes out of that in the whole theater. Do it for twenty seconds before you go to sleep. And note the dreams that come out of it.

This end point troubled me. Robert intuitively worked to bring the two characters together to create their world of interaction, a wise move in a two-character play. But when Alan held these images

together they seemed to describe a different problem: a sense that acting on the stage was unrealized. To what would Alan's dreams
respond? Would the autonomous imagination react to the actor's difficulty in getting onstage and feeling fulfilled? Would it react to the
world of the two characters that Robert had worked to create? Are
these questions inextricably linked or at loggerheads? To which, if
anything, would the dreams respond? I knew that this was an important moment for us that might reveal information that we did not
have about the process, but mostly I was worried.

When we moved on to Anthony Arkin's incubation, he moved
freely between his stage reality and his present, imagined reality.
When he accessed his performance text it had little of the quality of
being observed from without. It felt like the reflexive and constructive imaginations were at work together and very much part of the
scene as it unfolded in the imaginary landscape. To a large degree
Anthony stayed focused on his imaginative reality using his performance text only as a point of reference.

Robert began,

So what is the scene that you want to work on?

It took me a long time to figure out. I don't really have difficulty at
the moment. But there is a moment that is not as realized as it could
be. It is around the same time as the tent's construction. My character
takes the imaginary tent instructions off the tent and reads them.
This is a new level of commitment to the unconscious or to insanity
that this character makes, and it really is the final one.

You are standing or sitting? How do you imagine yourself there?

Well, this moment encompasses a few minutes in the play. I am
standing the whole time. It comes after a frightening shock. I cross to
center stage and stand there, holding the instructions.

Still in the mood of the shock?

Yes, it has catapulted me onto center stage.

Can you describe the mood?

Yeah. It is startled like a cat. But also, simultaneously focused and almost calmed into having to do something that cannot be done.

How does it feel in your body to be startled like a cat?

It feels nimble, agile, strong, energized.

And what is the moment like when you stop center stage? How does it feel in your body?

A coming to rest. It is tied into a timing element in me. It is the appropriateness of coming to rest on the stage.

Can you feel that coming to rest in your body?

Yes.

What happens to that startled response at this time?

It is nice to be able to ignore how frightening that was and to focus on somethingnew, which is the instructions. It is a way not to be scared any more.

Do you still know that you are scared?

There is an underlying panic, but it is at a high, continual pitch at this point.

Is it something that you hear?

No, it is more of a muscle vibration, a hair-trigger feeling.

Can you stay with the muscles in your body?

Yes.

What condition are they in?

Loose, actually. Not tense. The kind of looseness that makes you free to do anything at any moment.

And you can feel the panic?

Yes, somewhat behind the physical reality.

And now you begin to make a movement toward the imaginary directions?

I have them in my hand already.

And are they imaginary, or have they become real?

They are both.

And in the process of these few minutes are they becoming very real?

Yes.

Can you go to the point when they are still imaginary?

Yes, when I hold them up in front of my face to look at them.

And what do you see?

I see my two fists.

And how are you holding your two fists?

About seven or eight inches apart. Thumbs up as if on either side of the paper.

But it is still "as if"?

Yes.

And between your hands there is now what?

Air and an attempt to create the piece of paper.

What is it like in your body to feel that attempt? Feel it in your body. How does that attempt happen in your body?

I feel it in my shoulders and a concentration between my eyes.

Concentrate on that point between your eyes. What is taking place there?

An attempt to focus on something that isn't there. An attempt to conjure words, to see words that are there.

Can you say again what is happening in your shoulders?

Yes, I feel a bit hunched up and strong. My left shoulder is forward. Right shoulder is raised slightly. It is a stance.

How is it in your legs, that stance, before it becomes entirely real?

I don't know why—they feel skinny.

This is the first completely new experience given by the autonomous imagination.

Stay with the skinny feeling in your legs.

Robert pauses while Anthony does so.

What is it like to have skinny legs, strong shoulders that are hunched, and concentration in your forehead, trying to make the words become real?

It feels kind of top-heavy.

Stay with that top-heavy sense and slowly move to the point when there is a transition from imaginary to real. Is there any moment when you begin to feel it between your fingers?

Yeah.

Can you go to that moment?

Yeah.

What changes in your hands as it is now between your fingers?

They don't have to hold it that tightly.

Is it thin paper or thick paper?

It is medium quality paper, like computer paper. A manual—like you would get in a box.

A single page?

That changes, actually.

Tell me about how it changes.

When I take it off the tent it sounds like it is wrapped in plastic, as instructions are when they are taped in plastic bags to packages. And sometimes it is a single sheet of paper, badly Xeroxed. Then it generally becomes a couple of pieces folded over and stapled.

And as that happens is that also an increase of reality?

Yes.

Can you slowly move from the one page and your hands that are a little bit more relaxed, to the point where it becomes two stapled pages? Can you feel that transition in your hands?

Yes.

What happens in the rest of your body as the reality of the paper becomes thicker?

My body relaxes.

What happens to the point between your eyes?

That relaxes too. I have made the decision that this is possible.

Do you make the decision, or is it made in you?

It is made in me.

Can you go to the moment when it is made in you? What happens there?

Yeah, I want to help. I want to be available.

What changes in your interior being as the decision is being made in you that this is real?

That things are going to go better. That the other person and I are now on the same wavelength. I am relieved not to be accused of things and yelled at for a while. It is nice.

This was an interesting moment in which Anthony moved fluidly between reflexive ("That things are going to go better"), constructive ("That the other person and I are now on the same wavelength"), and autonomous ("It is nice") realms of imagination. "It is nice" had the striking simplicity of spontaneous revelation. Robert brought him deeper into his vision by directing him back to present sensate experience.

How do your legs feel?

They feel a little more capable, a little stronger. They feel pretty agile.

Can you see the man who is constructing the tent?

Yes.

Does he change as the reality increases?

He becomes less of a threat. Now he is almost somebody who needs to be taken care of. He is more fearful.

Can you look at him when he is still a threat? How is it conveyed to you that he is a threat to you?

Irrationality. Not listening. Not allowing the job to go the right way.

Robert has asked Anthony to make too great a leap. By asking, "Can you look at him when he is still a threat?" he's called for a circumstance that Anthony has not yet seen in the imagined reality. This might have worked, but the objectivity in Anthony's voice reveals that he is no longer in his imagination but recounting historical information. Robert redirects him back into an embodied present.

He is kneeling?

Yes.

Can you feel with your body what is going on with him?

Yes. That it is hard work he's doing.

Can you feel the hard work?

Yeah.

What is it like to be doing such hard work?

It is a strain on the back, but it's also productive. Productive, hard work feels good.

Now what is the moment like when the two of you are on the same wavelength?

A relief.

What is it like to suddenly be in the same state of being?

It feels more knowing, but also the weight of responsibility is heavier.

Can you say more about that weight of responsibility?

Yes, it feels older, more mature, troubled. It makes me feel haggard.

What is it like to be in such a haggard body?

Tension.

Where?

In the shoulders.

Similar or different than before when you hunched your shoulder, making it real?

The tension in the shoulders here is anxiety rather than the possibility of having to go into action.

Can you feel into that anxiety in the shoulders?

Yes. It hurts a little. It's more a soreness. It brings them up higher.

How does it feel to be so anxious in the shoulders?

It doesn't feel good but it feels wiser. It's a man of many responsibilities who is carrying it through, however difficult, painful, or scary.

Is there some kind of internal maturation process that takes place in these two minutes?

Yes.

Robert works slowly through the next progression.

OK, let's go first back to the moment when you are very concentrated in your forehead and it's not yet real, you feel in your hands that they are tight . . . Your shoulders are hunched, you are top-heavy, your legs are skinny . . . Now go to the moment when there is one page and beginning to get real, beginning to relax . . . Then when it becomes two pages it is more real . . . Then you look at the older man on his knees, who is at first threatening, and then you are on the same wavelength. You have a haggard feeling. Do you feel that?

Yes.

And then you begin to feel the anxiety in the shoulders, and you feel the anxiety and the wisdom in the anxiety. That is a long incubation.

Robert was right; that was a long incubation. The preparation of the incubation images and the number of images to recall before bedtime were both long. I didn't like it. There was something appealing to me about keeping the process streamlined. We already had proof that even the shortest incubation or a snapshot dream yielded what was necessary. A streamlined process makes it easier for actors, teachers, or other dreamworkers to undertake the technique on their own. The incubations Robert prepared with the Arkins were anything but. Practically, I was concerned that there was simply too much stuff for Anthony to incubate. Would he sleep? Would he be able to assimilate all of that sensate, imaginative information? I also felt that we were heading into a kind of complexity that only a highly trained psychoanalyst could master. I did not have the sense of "Do not practice without a license," but rather "You need a license to pull this off." We were not committing malpractice, but we might be conducting an experiment that could not be reproduced by others.

On the other hand, there were some new things that happened with the Arkins that excited me. This was the first time we ever incubated a very linear progression—the increasing reality of the paper. I was delighted that a progressive issue that needs to be addressed in the play had become the focus of the work. Anthony sought an increasing reality to the objects he handled. Robert addressed this progression quite simply, with patience and sensitivity.

Robert incorporated *both* characters into both incubation images in new ways. Granted, in the scene in *The Seagull* in which Treplev lays the seagull at Nina's feet, Linda's incubation brought Treplev's muddy shoes into the incubation image. But the sensate data were what Linda felt in her body when she saw the shoes. Here Robert did two different things. He went one step further with Anthony and had him transit into DeRecha's body, then brought him back to sense his own. More radically, he asked Alan to hold the two characters together and see what body emerged.

I hoped it would clarify that the interaction between DeRecha and Lefty changes both characters in some way that is critical to each going on his journey. Observing from the outside, Alan and Anthony's incubations helped solidify their mutual reality and something about their characters' throughlines. It started suggesting to me the hold DeRecha had on Lefty, what kept him in the warehouse, and what—if any—promise he held out to the young man. And vice versa. All of these were underlying ingredients that scored the unfolding action. In *Virtual Reality* the union of the two characters creates every moment on an almost empty stage. In preparing the incubation images in these ways Robert created an imaginative sphere in which the actor held both characters together so that both could operate on the other. The goal was to find out how these two particular characters make it possible for this story to unfold. Would it work for the actors? It was certainly the most complex incubation we had tried to date.

We left the Arkins and returned in two weeks.

I arrived at Alan's house and he told me that he'd dreamt four dreams since we'd last met. He felt that three of them were clearly connected to the incubation image. The fourth seemed on the surface not to be about the play at all; however, once he began thinking about it, he suddenly realized the connection. Alan stopped analyzing it, leaving the work to the process.

Robert and Anthony arrived and we began work. After reviewing

Alan's four dreams briefly, Robert selected the dream about Stravinsky (which follows) primarily because it is a story about an older man talking of a younger man. He then checked in with me for my opinion. I suggested the fourth dream, in part because Alan had de-selected it, but also because it offered the most direct example of a relationship developed between the two characters in which their presences and decisions affected each other, creating the relationship, as happens in the play.

Alan recounted the two dreams we chose.

> I am lying naked with "X," an actress I've known and worked with in life. We have been friends since the moment we met and have a loving and open relationship. In the dream we are talking and laughing and fondling each other like children. It suddenly turns sexual. This transition is very subtle but clear and we share an unspoken recognition of it. There is a tacit realization on both of our parts that if we go further, something in our relationship will be lost. Freedom of some kind. We will go into some place where we have rights and obligations with one another. It will turn into some form of bondage. We think twice before we proceed. I believe we decide not to consummate the relationship.
>
> I was sure this had no possible connection to the play. Then I remembered that she had once told me a story her (somewhat controlling) mother. And I thought, "Jesus! That is an exact analogy to Anthony's and my relationship onstage." Add to that the fact that I am directing! I have to be careful not to have one eye on him at all times.

The following is Alan's dream about Stravinsky:

> I am at a lecture where Stravinsky is talking. It becomes clear that he is talking about the laws of karma. He speaks about a young man

going off on an adventure, and that the parents—who are sharing the son's enthusiasm—should not just think of it as an idyll, but rather as an opportunity to heal an ancient problem. I am amazed that he is so aware, and start giving him a great deal of credit. But then I intuitively look at his face. The set of his mouth is in a sneer and is judgmental, angry. I back away from giving him too much respect.

Robert began.

Do you mind doing both dreams? Let's begin with the one about "X." Where does this take place?

I haven't got a clue.

What do you see as a setting?

Outdoors. *Alan gestures out the window.* Like that setting.

Is it warm?

Yes, it is comfortable. Very comfortable.

And is the sun shining?

I think so.

There is a lot of light?

Yes.

And you are both naked?

Yes.

And you have been naked for a long time together, or is the sense that it just began?

It doesn't feel like terribly long. Maybe twenty minutes.

What is the body position you are in?

We are both on our sides, facing each other.

And you are on which side?

I think I am on my left side.

What are your physical sensations as you lie there?

Great comfort, ease, and pleasure. Connection, a childlike connection.

And can you say something more about that childlike element?

Free of encumbrances of any kind. No agendas, other than our own pleasure and enjoyment of one another.

How does your skin feel?

Tingly and alive.

Is there conversation going on?

Yes, a lot of joking and laughing. We are wrestling playfully, but with a minimum of physical activity.

Can you go to the moment when a decision has to be made?

The degree of pleasure we are having with one another that becomes so spontaneous and connected that we recognize that it has become sexual.

Can you feel that kind of spontaneity?

Yes.

What kind of effect does it have on your body to be so spontaneous?

It feels enormously relaxing, loving, and connected.

What happens to that feeling when the decision is made that you shall not continue?

It turns into a slight sadness, a slight heaviness.

Can you say more about that heaviness?

Robert directs Alan to the physical sensation in which the emotion will naturally be embodied.

"Back to reality" is the phrase that comes to mind, although I don't know what I mean by that. Back to being an adult. Responsible. A recognition of who I really am, who we really are. I prefer it the other way.

Can you compare these two feelings, the one of being a child and the one of being a man?

The childlike feeling is better.

How is it different?

It is unconcerned with responsibility. It is less weighted, lighter. It's happier.

Now can you look at her lying on her right side?

Yes.

And her moods mirror yours?

Yes, they seem to.

And what of her movements can you actually see?

She is quite still at the moment. She seems to be taking the lead from me.

Can you sense into her stillness and her waiting for the man to take the lead?

Yes.

What is it like, that waiting for the man to take the lead?

It's exciting. Anticipatory, exciting, vulnerable.

What kind of sense of body is that excited, anticipatory vulnerability?

It feels very womanly. Particularly open from the waist down. Open and available in a very pure sense. Available to the reality around her. Hmm . . . interesting, interesting.

What did you just see?

There are things I have been consciously struggling with myself for the past weeks just before I go onstage, and sometimes on the stage.

Alan does not step out of this moment to observe it; he seems fully in his body in the present. Robert pauses to allow this reflection to open into awareness.

Can you feel into that openness in her lower body?

Yes.

What is it like to be so open in the lower body?

It feels wonderful. My fear is that it would feel castrated—but it doesn't. It feels more present, more available than I have ever known myself to be. More accessible and freer. It's really interesting.

What is she feeling in her upper body?

A lot of openhearted love.

What happens to her body when she notices that Alan makes the decision to stop?

Slightly sad, but understanding.

What happens to her lower body especially?

It gets heavier.

What is happening to the receptivity of the lower body?

It is feeling lonely and incomplete.

Feel that transition from the fully open lower body to the one that feels incomplete and sad. Describe the sense of that transition—how it happens. Feel into the moment of the transition.

Alan pauses for while, then continues.

A shutting down of possibilities. Wistful and yearning. Although—it is not a tragic thing; it is just slightly sad. It is interesting, because even though things are not taking place the way she would like them to, they are taking place the way they are supposed to. I can only assume that the correct consummation, whatever that means, is going to transpire one way or another. That it will be OK.

Now, can you for a moment feel back into her openness and then to the heaviness? Can you go back and forth?

Yes.

Feel that transition that comes from rational decision on Alan's part?

Yes, I can.

All right. Now let's go to the other dream. We will come back to this. You see Stravinsky where?

It is an intimate lecture hall. He is quite close. There are not terribly many people in the audience.

This is Stravinsky at what age?

His sixties. My age.

What of this lecture do you actually remember now?

None of it.

What do you remember?

I remember the tone—the adventure sounded like it would be very exciting. A journey anyone would be excited to embark upon.

Can you feel into the excitement of that tone?

Yes.

And how does it make your body feel to get into the excitement of that tone?

Healthy, youthful, strong, filled with anticipation—a sense of hope, promise, and adventure.

And what is that like in your muscles?

Invigorating. It makes them feel very potent and loose.

Now look at Stravinsky's face, and you discover the sneer. Can you sense into that sneer? What is it like to sneer like that?

It is not as bad as it looks. It is just a recognition of the pain that the journey is going to represent, that nobody is acknowledging. It will not be as carefree as everyone thinks it will—it will be arduous.

And he knows this from his own experience?

Yes.

Can you sense into his experience that tells him this will be arduous?

It's the extraordinary effort he has put into his work. His genius, his
lack of recognition in connection with what he knows to be his abilities, lack of money.

Stay with that for a moment.

The goal of Robert's "Stay with that for a moment" is to allow Alan's
awareness to develop in his body while seeing the image in his mind's
eye. Robert then takes him back into the unfolding landscape of the
dream.

Can you sense back into the younger man who is just setting out on
the journey? Stravinsky is on a later point in the journey having had
many experiences. Can you feel into the young man and then back
into Stravinsky? Can you feel the contrast between them?

I sure can.

What's it like to be in the contrast, to feel the contrast between these
two men? When you move back and forth between the man who is
young, exuberant, whose muscles are strong, feels potent, whose
world is just going to start—and the older man who . . .

They are both crazy. The only reconciliation is a synthesis of both
things.

Alan moves to an interpretation, and Robert redirects him back to
sensate experience once again.

Why don't you just try this, each one discretely. First feel the younger
man in your body, and now feel the older man in your body.

OK.

And feel what these two bodies are like. What is it like to embody
both of them?

A long pause ensues as Alan does so.

It is wonderful.

Can you describe what you are feeling?

Yeah, when I feel them both simultaneously I get the sense of exuberance and future, hope—tempered by an awareness that it can be precarious. The precariousness and dangers involved temper the exuberance without dampening it. It is not fearful, but injects a cautionary tone into the experience. The search for meaning will be resolved internally, not with as much external excitement as the younger man seeks.

And what kind of body are you in now? What are the physical sensations?

It is slower but very strong. I still have the strength of youth but tempered. The slowness gives it a kind of power.

Can you feel into that particular slowness?

Yes.

Can you stay with that feeling?

Yes.

OK, now we are going to go back to the transition in "X" from the childlike feelings and the openness in the lower body to the heaviness of closing up.

OK.

What is it like to have those feelings together? The older man with the younger man in him and the lower body that is open and then experiences the heaviness of closing up?

It is wonderful. It feels wonderful.

Describe as many elements as you can since it is anchored in your body.

I feel strong, in control of myself. I feel a sense of unity—all the parts feel united. I feel unaccustomed joy at being who I am. I feel air flowing into me, in lower areas of myself. Air flows into places I do not ordinarily let things flow. I am complete, an entity unto myself, without needing anything external to complete me. It's liberating.

Do you think you can get back to this body feeling you have right now?

Yes. I have been working on it for thirty years and I feel as I am just touching on it now for the first time.

It seems to be possible to get there through feeling the lower body of "X," and feeling the combination of the older man and his experience and his lack of recognition, and the younger man with his exuberance. Those elements together seem to bring about this world.

Anthony Arkin's Dreams
Anthony had four dreams. The following are the two we selected.

I don't normally remember my dreams, so recalling four is pretty good for me. Some of these had a quality unlike any dream I have ever had.

Amelia [Anthony's wife] and I are looking all over a big hotel complex for a place to have sex. There are too many people, too much family. The number of family members everywhere makes it impossible. Our cat, Simon, sheds a lot. I look at my thumb and there is a white hair or whisker lying across it. Then I realize that it is driven through my thumb, like a piece of wheat driven through a tree by the force of a tornado. I pull it out like a thorn.

This next was a weird dream. A good one.

I am on a vast ship with my family. It is a tanker or carrier. I can't see the ocean. Millions of rooms, streets, warehouses. I am afraid of flying, and that's perhaps why I am on the ship. My dad is the captain of the ship and the family is the crew. Amelia is on the boat and we just got married. We hadn't had a honeymoon yet. I say to Dad, "Can we have a few days off and get off the boat?" He snaps, ornery, "You already had a wedding party," and sends us back to work.

In the next scene my brother Adam, actor Richard Mazer, a group of other people, and I are all in the woods. We are hunting down a homicidal maniac in order to kill him. He's tracking us at the same time. Spooky, but entertaining, too. I complain to Adam about Dad's being unfair about the honeymoon. I am also wondering who the maniac will kill. The killer is like the villain in the Halloween movies so I figure his next victim will be Richard Mazer since he's a character actor.[1]

The "captain" dream is clearly germane; the relationships are analogous to the play and the incubation. There is also something relevant about Anthony's thumb penetrated by the cat's hair. DeRecha penetrates Lefty. I find the image dense and difficult to grasp—which snags my interest. I recall Anthony saying that he had catlike agility in the moment before the imaginary incidents of the play begin to take on an increased reality.

Robert enters the dreamwork at a place where Anthony feels most relaxed, in which the imagery is inviting.

> Let's go to the hotel dream first. It starts with a mood of trying to make love?

---

1. To clarify: it is standard practice in horror and science fiction films for the first character who dies to be a character actor, never a principal. The audience is invested in the character's humanity and so suffers his loss, but it leaves the protagonist alive to save the day.

Yes.

Where is it taking place?

It seems to be a hotel. Out of season. Mostly populated by my family. It's supposed to be jovial and friendly. It is dimly lit.

You are walking around trying to find a room?

Yes, it is Felinniesque, a party atmosphere. We're wandering around from room to room and there are people everywhere.

Is there mounting frustration?

Yeah, but there is also humor.

Your wife's response?

We're having fun together. The atmosphere is a little creepy, but we're having fun together.

Can you sense into that creepy atmosphere?

It's cold, dimly lit. There is chatter everywhere. The place is not dirty or old, but it reminds me of cobwebs, though there aren't any. It's either an old place or a new one that is recently run-down.

Are you holding her hand?

Yes. The primary thing is that we're together.

Can you feel into this sense of togetherness and the longing to consummate it?

Yes. I feel younger and giddier. We are dashing around. There seems to be wind blowing her shawl. We have to make small talk with people and then get out of these encounters as quickly as possible. We dash down the hall. It feels youthful.

At what point does the scene with the hair come up?

It feels like an epilogue to the dream. I don't know where it is.

You have a sense that the hair has grown through your thumb.

Yeah. At first I think it's resting on it but then on closer inspection—

Can you sense inside your thumb and the tugging on the hair?

It's not painful, but I anticipate that it will hurt. It is very unusual. I can feel the tugging on my flesh.

Can you focus all your senses—concentrate on your thumb—and feel how the hair is through your thumb, tugging?

Yes, my body feels like vomiting, purging, cleansing. Unnatural, though.

Stay with your feeling in your thumb, tugging at it, and let it go through your body.

It's actually sort of sexual; a release of pressure and negativity.

What's happening in your body as the negativity is released?

Relaxing. Relaxing.

Robert moves to the "captain" dream without any introduction or transition.

Where do you approach your father?

On the deck of the ship. I smell ocean air.

Can you smell it?

Almost.

Your wife is not with you?

No, not while I ask.

What is he doing?

Working. I am waiting for a good moment to talk.

What's his authority? He's the captain. Is there trepidation in going up to him?

Yes, anxious, nervousness in my stomach. I am fairly confident that he'll say yes. It is a beautiful day, we've all worked hard. I deserve a couple of days off. He is surly and bombastic, the kind of person you'd be nervous approaching.

Is this captain a character in your dream or is he your father?

He's a character. Not like my father is in life.

Does the nervousness in your belly increase as you approach him?

Yes, I am almost stammering.

Can you feel into your almost stammering voice toward the captain?

It's embarrassing.

Stay with that voice. What happens when his response is so negative?

My tension goes away. I feel resignation, disappointment, and anger. I feel my face get flushed.

Can you feel the shift from nervousness into anger and resignation?

It's like a melting; a slow revolution.

Is he more you father or captain or both?

More captain.

Can you describe the look on the captain's face?

Distracted. It's probably a bad time to ask. His blanket refusal and dismissal of me is immediate. Its implication is that I am shiftless and lazy for asking. His arms gesture at all the work that remains to be done.

Can you feel into the gesture and his immediate "No?"

Yes, but I can also sense that he has a point; there is a lot to do.

Can you fell how distracted he is, how much there is to do, and here is Anthony, asking for some time for a honeymoon?

The dismissal isn't personal. He is not angry with Anthony. It feels correct and strong to say no for the betterment of the ship.

Can you feel the responsibility for the ship?

Yes. It is not too much to handle, but it's at the limit.

Can you feel into his whole body—the gesturing arms, so much to do?

Yes. It feels wiry and strong.

Stay with that. . . . Now go to Anthony's melting. . . . Now go to the purging hair pulled through your thumb. Try to stay with these three body feelings: the melting, the purging, and the strong wiriness. What is it like to feel these three feelings?

Exhilarating.

Can you say what's happening to your body now?

It's an interesting combination of weak and strong, releasing and tension.

Stay with these three feelings. What is it like to stay in this body?

It feels healthy, but it also feels restless. I should do something with this body!

With this body you should go onstage. Start out with being with your wife because you feel safe in your togetherness. Then feel into your thumb. Feel the cleansing and wrenching. Then go to the moment that Anthony is standing in front of the captain, melting. Then go into the captain and his wiry, strong body and sense of responsibility.

Not to mince words, I will say that I found the level of complexity that the first and second steps of the dreamwork had reached with the Arkins upset me. Robert's journey with Alan and Anthony was a confrontation to me. Robert took them places that I had neither intuitively understood in the moment nor felt I could reproduce in the future.

Robert asked the Arkins to hold separate characters or moments together to create a third body-self. Not only that, but in the second phase he worked freely between two dreams and asked the Arkins to hold together characters or images from different dreams to create a new embodied entity. In the past we had asked actors to transit into other characters and experience that new body. We'd directed Linda to hold together images of (*The Seagull*'s) Nina in her father's home and Nina at Sorin's home across the lake as an incubation image, but they were two aspects of the same character. Never before had we held two disparate characters together to create a third thing, and never before had we worked freely between dreams.[2] I was a good dreamworker, yet it would likely not have occurred to me to ask the actor to inhabit both characters and then hold the images together to create the relationship. Admittedly, a part of my defensiveness against

---

2. Actually, this statement is not true. When Robert and I had worked on my dream for *The Illusion* he had me hold Alcandre and Lyse together to create the oppositional state between them. But at the time when we dreamworked the Arkins I didn't recall that instance, both because it was my dream and because it was a director's dream. At the time, simply holding them together in the same sphere during the incubation was so consciously informative that I let the information slip from memory. Another good reason to observe the process when I intend to write about it!

it as an idea lay there. For the first time I felt a little left in the dust by Robert's experience with dreams and psychoanalysis. It was not a salubrious feeling.

On a less personal note, we had already had such success with a simpler approach. Just what was this new complexity going to accomplish that simplicity would not offer? The technique as practiced before worked. It solved problems. It created body-worlds. It opened the actor into autonomously operative imagination. It was utterly surprising and produced starling results. The utilitarian (and poetic) nature of what we'd done prior to coming to the Arkins was clear to me. If the dreamwork process retained its mystery (as it always will) I could at least readily understand how to practice both the cause and effect sides of it. That translated into being able to do it easily. I believed that after reading a few chapters of this book, perceptive and patient (with process) artists in the theater community could undertake the dreamwork themselves with every expectation of doing it fairly well the first time out. But this new stuff was different.

So let us step back and look at what happened with the Arkins because it proved important and powerful. Let's put the new elements of the process into a context. Together, let's both see if we can formalize what happened in this session so that we understand it and can practice it. And in the final analysis, if the work done here treads too convoluted a path for the reader's tastes, then there are simpler approaches that we have already detailed.

Background: Alan had three acting agendas going into our session.[3] When I first spoke to him he mentioned wanting to incubate a

---

3. In *The Actor Speaks*, Alan Arkin confessed another agenda entirely. It was nothing less than to subvert gloriously the Stanislavsky system by deploying unfettered imagination that worked far outside of Stanislavsky's structures. The first time he worked with his own agenda, he said, "[It] made me feel like an acting criminal" (p. 79). But it worked seamlessly and hilariously, and he hasn't stopped experimenting.

dream that would get him happily on stage. Instead, he chose to incubate the moment when DeRecha and Lefty construct the tent. His aim was to give it more reality. Alan had a third, unspoken goal, which he only referred to after he had walked through his dream landscape. He called it, "one of my primary agendas for my acting," and it was to incorporate male and female principles. He wanted both receptiveness and action, along with the other attributes he associated with each gender, and he wanted them in the same body. He later told us that he was frustrated every night in his attempt to achieve this before going on stage. He said that metaphorically "ripping away" at his lower body each night was not achieving the desired result of "uncovering the feminine." Three conscious agendas in varying stages of being forefronted and backgrounded are a fair number. Writing, directing, and acting in a play with his son compounded Alan's field of experience further. Imagine that all of these things, and more, add up to Alan Arkin in this moment. If that is the case then the dreams that Alan Arkin has will be seeded by his concerns. All of them. That certainly was the case.

Robert and I always approached the incubation image as if it were the seed that contained the genetic whole; nothing about it was extraneous to the DNA. But with the Arkins he ramped up this commitment and altered the practice accordingly. If the seeding incubation image still contains all of the genetic material of the parent (the actor intersecting with the play) then the dream offspring (the character intersecting with the actor) could only be comprised of the genetic material that went into its making. With the Arkins Robert worked with the assumption that there was no such thing as daytime detritus being recycled meaninglessly in dreams—*everything was relevant to the dreamer,* the play and the seed. In other words, as in a dream, everything is comprised of the dreamer, so everything *is* the dreamer. Robert asked the two men to hold images of two (or more) people together. He considered each an aspect or a state of the actor or character segregated from the other as they are in dreams. When unified they created a whole. Notice that the images are often contrasting: youth and age, experience and innocence, masculine and feminine.

Robert began incubating by taking Alan first into DeRecha's body, kneeling, and next into the tentlike, canvas body, where he felt safe, whole, permeable, and unified. From that place of comfort, he directed his attention to Lefty. "What kind of body comes from that sense of the spoken (annoying and eager to please) voice?" This question prompted Alan into transiting into Lefty's body, where he discovered a feeling of strength and integration. Robert asked Alan to contrast the man (DeRecha) on his knees with this young man, to which Alan responded that the younger man had innocence. Going back through the safety of the tentlike body, Robert asks Alan to hold both images together. What emerged when he held together "these two different ways of feeling" was big, expansive, hopeful, warm, anticipatory—but unrealized.

As I said earlier, I thought this last image pertained directly to Alan's initial statement about wanting to get joyfully onto the stage. But Alan's autonomous imagination proved otherwise. His dreams rebounded with exquisite stories about everything the actor had on his mind. They were as much about the play and the characters as they were about directing in that complex field of experience; they spoke to Alan's desire for a unification of feminine and masculine principles, but they also took him to the brink of his dissatisfaction with stage acting. It was all there and they were inseparable. And, because acting can be said to be the ongoing meeting of the actor and the character with the other actor and character, all things personal, professional, and artistic were at play in all aspects of the field. Each part of the dream narrative was a metonym, a piece standing for the whole. Although I was startled when Robert chose to draw images from both dreams, in hindsight I understand. They were two dreams generated by the identical seed. The fact that neither Alan nor Anthony had difficulty embodying images from two different dream landscapes in one session testifies to the genetic match. Zero rejection.

Robert found the relaxed, easy place to enter into Anthony's dream landscape through Anthony's relationship with his wife. Coming from that place, he asked Anthony to hold together the body-selves of Anthony melting in front of the captain (dream two), the purging of the cat hair pulled through his thumb (dream one), and the strong, wiriness of the captain's body (dream two). Another way of looking at this is that Robert asked Anthony to hold together one image that on the surface had only to do with Anthony, one of himself in relation to the captain, and one of the captain "alone". When he did so Anthony felt exhilarated. He told us that this new body was an interesting combination of weak and strong, release and tension that led him to declare, "I should do something with this body!" And indeed, from Anthony's report of how things went the following weeks in performance, that body knew just what to do.

Two weeks later I spoke with both Anthony and Alan on the phone. This was the first time I had not been present in the theater working with the actors to evoke the dreams while working on the play. Did it require the outside assistance of a director or dream-worker? We had no idea.

Anthony reported the following.

> How the dreamwork process works is a total mystery to me. That it did something is indisputable.
>
> The dreamwork made total visceral sense. It resonated physically and emotionally throughout my body, and made greater emotional sense out of the character, and where he would be at certain points. The cat's hair growing out of my thumb, for example, was such an unnatural sensation and experience and it corresponded precisely to the unnaturalness of the situation Lefty finds himself in.
>
> In the beginning, for about a week to ten days, I brought the

images to bear for about five to ten minutes before going onstage. I am used to meditating and I found it easy to visualize. But I was surprised by how extreme the physiological and emotional reactions to the visual images were long after the sessions in which we broke down the dreams. For example, I felt intense electricity in my spine every time I did it. I tried not to be analytical about what to use, or how it might work. I just trusted that something would happen.

The first night I did the preparation was the most emotionally exhausting performance I have ever done in my life. The dreamwork somehow injected a huge amount of information, but it was embryonic and unformed. I knew I'd have to wrestle it into control, but I'd exposed places I had never exposed before. I was in a fairly unusual situation for any actor to find himself in. I was acting in a two character play with my father, who was also its writer and director. Just being directed by your father for the first time is an experience in which a great deal goes unsaid—as you'd imagine. But the night of that performance an enormous amount of emotion and behavior flooded out, and it definitely needed some sculpting.

So the next day, after a good night's sleep, I realized I couldn't bring quite that weight to the play in the next performance. It wasn't right for the tone, and the whole thing was so loaded. I did the preparation again, but this time I cultivated the dream images with more of sense of humor. It's hard to explain. I think I just took it much lighter and I combined them more specifically with the intention of going out onstage.

The impact was similar; elating, actually, but definitely not exhausting. Since then my performance has changed dramatically. In fact, my father and I are working in ways that change exponentially, rather than linearly. So much of my ego resistance dropped and each night we find out more and more about what the play is about. It has become much more of a collaboration. And parenthetically, it enabled me to take his direction with much greater ease.

I took the whole sequence through from beginning to end, ending with embodying the captain. First of all the sequence makes intuitive and physical sense, but also ending with the captain keys me
much more into relating to my father's character, DeRecha. Lefty
needed to walk onto the stage with a sense of male security, and I
derived a real feeling of muscularity and responsibility from the captain. I started feeling truly secure; tough people don't have to prove
that they are expecting a fight and can deal with it. They are just
secure and tough in themselves.

Of course, my father did give me one direction that made me
feel like I was in Acting 101. He suggested that Lefty can't walk in
expecting a problem. "Duh." That direction combined with the
dreamwork has created a state in which I am more comfortable. And
the more comfortable I am in coming in to do the job initially, the
crazier DeRecha's requests seem.

But like my father, the dreamwork did not specifically affect the
moment we incubated, even though it helped in much more sweeping
ways. Actually, it made it easier for me to find the moment to take a
direction my father gave me weeks before. He asked me to reach into
my pocket at some point and eat the imaginary nuts DeRecha had
given me. But I never found the moment. Then one day it just fell
into place. DeRecha puts the invisible crate down on the floor, and it
lands with a crash that is a real, amplified sound effect. I jump back,
startled. Then he tells me to find the directions and read them. One
night in the past two weeks I found myself reaching into my pocket
and grabbing those imaginary nuts and eating a few. It created a
bridge of virtual madness to reading those directions—and suddenly
it all became much realer.

Every night my father and I come off stage and ask each other,
"What *happened* out there? Was it the dreams?"

So far so good. I then called Alan. The first thing he said to me
was, "I didn't feel like anything happened. Nothing at all happened

around the building of the tent." With a sinking heart I told myself, "Well, I guess this will have the advantage of being the shortest phone conversation in history."

He went on.

Of course there were other dramatic results. I was excited to find the connective tissue between the incubation and the dreams. Even though [the image I'd embodied of] "X" remained an intellectual prospect when I tried to take on that body, something about working with the dreams each night has helped very much in integrating the masculine with the feminine. I have struggled with this for years and now it is taking place more rapidly. The idea of separating the two at this point in my life is ridiculous and divisive.

I also seem to have much greater compassion for my character now. He seems sad to me. I used to be judgmental about him, but now I feel his plight. I see that same compassion extending each night to Anthony's character as well. I feel compassion for our mutual plights. There is an ease between Anthony and me onstage now. I used to feel a personal loss when I was working with him. Now I feel that our characters are engaged in the same enterprise.

Anthony's work has been shot out of a cannon. I had a directorial idea for him—I felt that he came onstage anticipating trouble. It would be funnier and more appealing if he entered without anticipating anything adverse. So I don't know to what degree that direction had its effect as opposed to the dreamwork.

The actual way I am working seems to have shifted. Acting has always been a horizontal experience for me based in time. Action had to do with expediency and pressure on the character, which I took on. But it has nothing to do with me any more. I began thinking of the character without any urgency—even if *he* experiences extreme urgency. His actions stay the same, but I can tell it as a story without getting clenched in it.

As I said in an earlier chapter, no good technique should need the ongoing ministrations of an outside person. An actor must be able to locate the boundary to be explored of his own volition and to draw support for his imagination and his acting from that source.

As an experiment, this was more than fair. Not only did Robert and I not know the play well going in, but we were also in no way part of the production process. The effects of our absence were essential to assay. We relied upon the skill, technique, and talent of these professionals to use the dreamwork in their own ways. Time had made clear that people with little or no acting processes have difficulty making good use of the dreams, regardless of the precision, bearing, or great beauty the incubated dreams might contain. By virtue of their innate talent and acquired technique, the Arkins were ideal candidates for such a blind experiment.

This had shown us that individuals can easily adapt the technique. When the Arkins entered the theater, each deployed the dreamwork in his own fashion. The fact that the dreamwork's story is durable enough to withstand being encoded by each actor in his own private language without ministry from an outsider was most encouraging. This is the hallmark of a readily ascertained boundary where a good story is being told, and that yields a good technique.

It is provocative that the moments both Arkins chose to incubate were not changed by the dreamwork. Much deeper changes took place for them. While Robert's new, daring, and expansive way of working is responsible for the depth, I suspect it is also responsible for the failure to change the actors' initial choice of moment to incubate. I wonder what would have happened had we prepared these incubations and dreams more simply.

If the work with the Arkins was an objectively fair experiment, then the story I am about to recount is as loaded as a marked deck. I tell it because Robert continued to work by holding characters together to create a third entity and by working between dreams. I tell it because important information emerged about the nature of incubated dreams.

Robert and I wanted to brush up our technique before we headed for Los Angeles to work with the John Ruskin School. So I called Linda and Tara and asked them to pick a scene from a play to work on, and we'd incubate some dreams. As experimental procedures go this was really lousy. I had no intention of writing about this experience, so I did not record the whole process as a "lab report." Tara and Linda were part of the initial dreamwork experiment, and they both do the process easily and welcome the results. They share the same values and vocabulary as actors. I have directed them both for years, and have the inside track on what they think and feel. The actors have faith that both Robert and I are expert and accord us the trust that enables collaborators to produce beautiful work. And beyond all of that is the fact that we love one another. Put these all together and the fix is in.

Tara and Linda chose to work on the final scene of Fornes's play *Fefu and Her Friends*. It is a play they have thought about together for years but never performed. The work we did on *Fefu* transpired several weeks after the World Trade Towers collapsed, during the week that the plane crashed in Queens. Tara is from Queens, and her mother still lived there.

Fefu and Her Friends is symbolic realism. Briefly, it is the story of a group of accomplished, intelligent women, scholars and artists, who come to Fefu's home in the country in order to discuss an upcoming symposium. Fefu, the acknowledged leader of the group, is plagued by a sense of impending judgment and doom. She has always been aware that her husband finds her repulsive in some way, but she agrees with him. Women are, in their way, both loathsome and beautiful. Fefu accepts that. But somehow, lately, the scale has lost its balance, and Fefu finds herself dragged away from acceptance and toward excoriating judgment against the moist darkness that is part of being a woman.

Among the women at the house this weekend is Julia, a woman who was always effective in the world, a woman who had blazed through life with many of the qualities attributed to men. But in the recent past, while the men hunted deer on the grounds of Fefu's home, Julia had an encounter with her own repressed feminine side. During this encounter—delusional and symbolic yet with dire physical consequences—Julia is crippled and is confined to a wheelchair. In the dilated moment of the metaphysical accident, Julia hallucinates the voices of male judges who "let her live," in exchange for which she must abjure her feminine nature.

Fefu recognizes Julia as one who contends with the same forces that plague her. In the final scene of the play, Fefu has just seen Julia walk to get some sugar for her coffee. No one else has seen it. Julia is not even aware that she did it. Fefu implores Julia to stand with her against the male judges, to claim themselves as whole. Julia cannot. And in a final moment that resists logical description, Fefu fires a shotgun outdoors, killing a rabbit. At the same moment, Julia dies.

Robert developed the incubation images on the telephone a few days before we began work. He held images of both characters together. For example, Linda chose to incubate why it was important to her (Fefu) that Julia walks. The incubation image was drawn from Fefu's body *and* Julia's body as Linda imagined them.

We met in Boston. The women and I gathered in my office at MIT and we sat for an hour and a half to simply talk about the play, and that scene in particular. It was pretty astonishing how in the dark Tara and Linda were about the inner life of the play. Linda understood maybe 25 percent of what was going on with Fefu. Shockingly, Tara was totally mystified by Julia. It was as if they both had some kind of bizarre actor's amnesia blocking their normally acute intelligence. So I talked, and then we traced the events of the play to let them speak for themselves. In a play as densely symbolic as *Fefu*, it is important to see if there is a logical throughline that can be documented by what the characters say and do. Indeed there was a through-line, and Linda and Tara quickly made the intellectual connections. Linda began making some emotional connections while we sat, but Tara—? It was as if that part of her that could imagine her way into Julia's grievous circumstances were damaged. I led her through it in wee baby steps and we laughed together at how odd it was that it was even necessary. We headed for the rehearsal studio to begin working, which we did to good effect. We worked fast, each knowing that no words, actions, or silences would fall away unexplored.

A little sidebar of interest: when Robert arrived we immediately asked him, "How do men hate themselves?" In the play the women attribute all the self-loathing to their gender and see no commensurate negativity in men. He immediate answered, "Men doubt that they will measure up." We checked his answer against a couple of accomplished men in our own lives, and they both promptly said the same thing. This came as a relief to us and made us women not feel so all alone in a world of severe judgment.

Linda and Tara told us their dreams. Linda had three dreams and Robert chose an image from each dream. They were: an uploading of information into her brain and the feeling of her brain taking it all in; anger in her belly accompanied by a squaring of shoulders; and the excitement and whirling of ideas and words throughout her body.

Walking over to the rehearsal studio, Tara told me that she'd had only one dream and it was about the plane crash in Queens. Robert had spent the past two months doing volunteer work with people suffering nightmares as a result of the incidents of September 11, 2001. I told him about Tara's dream and he looked concerned. He felt that this was a posttraumatic dream and that it could be both too upsetting to incubate and not productive as far as *Fefu* was concerned. But given our long-standing relationship and mutual trust, we proceeded cautiously with the understanding that we would not explore anything that started seeming perilous.

Oddly, Tara worked with an ease that was surprising given the circumstances. I do not mean to say it was easy. The images that arose when she inhabited the dream landscape were horrible, and there were long pauses as she took them in. But she was not manifestly distressed. Her breathing stayed steady. Her face and body expressed unpleasantness but not present anguish. It took some time to walk through that landscape, but Robert and Tara completed the second phase of the process.

In the dream she was taking a pleasant after dinner stroll in Queens with a friend of hers. He was talking amicably, but no words came from his mouth. Suddenly, the earth split and voices screamed, "A plane crashed in Queens!" People rushed about her as the world was filled with sound. That was the end of the dream. When Robert and Tara entered the dream landscape they explored it carefully. Dozens of sensate details emerged. Tara reinhabited the sudden emergence of sound, the rent in the earth, and she even descended into the hole as part of the embodied landscape. We ended there for the day.

I picked Tara and Linda up at 11:00 A.M. the next morning. It seemed a bit daunting to rehearse the climax of a titanically symbolic play on a cold Sunday morning, especially in the light of the fact that we'd had an hour and a half total of rehearsal time. We'd all have been hesitant to enter that particular scene on a chilly Sunday morning at 11:00 A.M. if we were making the whole play! It is just one of those scenes. So we stalled, talked, and drank coffee and then screwed our courage to the sticking place and started work. Tara and Linda went deeper and deeper. I was amazed that we'd gotten to a quite grounded, interesting scene by the time Robert arrived.

I urged the women to resist performing for Robert, but they could not help themselves. The acting fell apart a bit, but the foundation of the work was solid. We had Tara reinhabit the embodied images from her dream. Robert and Tara took a minute or two for this and then we reminded her to simply let the images go. Linda

began the scene. By the end Tara-as-Julia was no longer merely pro-
tecting herself from the judges, she was trying desperately to shield
Fefu from them as well. She was shaking uncontrollably, sobbing in
terror and despair, and Linda-as-Fefu was sobbing in defeat. The
actors looked up in amazement at the transformation, only to see
Robert and me crying.

We debriefed for a minute and then had Linda reinhabit her
dream images. We were working fast. Here are Linda's words lifted
from an email she sent a friend.

> [H]e guides me through these images into a new physical body. I
> come out of it, let go of the body, and start the scene. The room is
> transformed. I am Fefu. The words are so sharp, so deep and painful.
> My objective and desires are crystal clear.
>
> The stakes are even higher. Now all of a sudden I know every
> minute bit of Fefu and Julia's history. I don't need to know my lines
> or try to recall them because I open my mouth and the words come. I
> need so much for Julia to fight because I want to live and I need her
> to help me live. By the end of the scene I am no longer begging for
> her not to give up, I am begging for my life.

I've got to tell you, this was the most astonishing thing I had ever
seen happen in a rehearsal, whether mine or anyone else's. Robert and
I were wracked with weeping. Fefu's desperation and terror fed Julia's,
and they were locked in a terrible, wild-eyed struggle. As Fefu lost
emotional control, Linda's body gave up autonomous control of her
tear ducts, salivary glands, and the mucous membranes of her nose.
As she begged for her life from Julia, fluids poured unobserved from
her nose, eyes, and mouth.

At no point did I stop the acting because I could see that there
was a supporting structure within these two actors I know so well.
But would I have been capable of stopping it, I wonder? In the grasp

of the characters' misery, I did not know where their interaction
would lead. Each moment was whole in itself and became Robert's
and my reality. Where else could I go when I was so engulfed? It was
like we all, the actors, the characters, the play, and the audience, were
being taken under and tumbled by an ocean wave. Robert and I wept
for these two characters, but also for the sheer pain of living.

Golly. It is difficult to explain this to the reader. It was just great
acting, and it came from two young women who had not rehearsed
the play, who were way off base when we talked the scene through
just twenty-four hours earlier. If one had a theater company, could
this kind of work be the standard it set? It was horribly beautiful.

As rotten an experimental model as it was, it proofed the yeast.
What seemed to Robert, an experienced analyst, to be a posttraumatic stress dream, like so many he'd dealt with recently, was not. Or
perhaps it both was and was not. What troubled Tara most about the
scene in *Fefu and Her Friends* seeded it. Indeed, she was suffering a New
Yorker's ripe terror. And Julia is suffering her own. The seed contained all of Tara's concerns both for the play and for herself, just as
Alan Arkin's incubation image and dreams ended up expressing his
three agendas. What emerged from the dream state carried the DNA
of both Tara and the play. New York was inseparable from Julia's
paralysis, the plane crash inseparable from Julia's horror at Fefu's
request to fight, and Tara's personal life became Julia's. In talking
about the technique of personalization, Stephen Spinella once said to
me, "My life is the character's opportunity." With the dreamwork
personalization takes on a new, cavernous depth that simultaneously
releases some of the most liberated acting I have ever seen.

CHAPTER NINE

Rules for Dreamworking the Character's Body

Although Robert suggested to me early on that we would ultimately produce the character's body via the dreamwork, I dismissed it out of hand. Not that I knew what we'd create, but I distrusted it as a grandiose, nontheatrical statement. My own initial goal was big enough—to access the wild sea of imagination. That this sea would shape itself into the character's body seemed hyperbole at worst, and wishful thinking at best.

It was immediately apparent that some kind of possession took place after we'd dreamworked the actor's body, and still I didn't consciously accept what was happening. Even while I *wrote* that Arkadina possessed Tara, I had not (really) heard myself. I was happy to declare that the God possessed the actor, but that was such an outrageous statement that I could make it gladly. I was not dissembling—the actors were possessed by *something*, the acting was radically altered. But still I did not see what was taking place. Yet as we dreamworked more and more actors' bodies, time and again I sat in the presence of act-

ing that evoked a qualitatively similarity, even though each performance was uniquely different.

After dreamworking, the character simply emerged. The actor
made way for his behavior, his psychic states, his history, his desires,
his worldview, and his imagination. Alan Arkin stated, "It has nothing to do with me any more. I began thinking of the character without any urgency—even if he experiences extreme urgency. His actions
stay the same, but I can tell it as a story without getting clenched in
it." Time and again, an ease descends on the actor and he can simply
trust that he participates in the voice you hear next, but it will not be
his.

Perhaps that is why it is more difficult to dreamwork actors who
consciously mine their own autobiographies as primary sources.
Their outrages, joys, and pains are lent to the character, and the synthesis between actor and character remains lively at the boundary
between the actor's emotional history and the character's event. These
actors experience working away from that boundary as "not truth."
The dreamwork banishes that boundary between, and places everything—the actor, the character, and the world of the play—inside a
sphere of imagination.

I submit to you that Robert was right: the dream is the character's dream, and the dreamworked body comprises the character's
body. I don't mean that the literal stance and gaze the actor assumes
when holding together the embodied images are the body, nor is it
Michael Chekhov's psychological gesture, nor Brecht's gestus. No,
these networked images are the symbolic body, and when they are
held together and then released, they fire up a brave, ongoing dialogue
that unfolds effortlessly in the acting, and then the character's body
materializes in the landscape. Like your body and mine, it is not
monolithic, but comprised of shifting body-worlds.

As we move from preparing the incubation image to preparing
the dreamworked body a major shift transpires. The actor begins out-

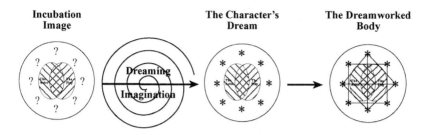

| Incubation
Image | | The Character's
Dream | The Dreamworked
Body |

side of the play and the character. Rehearsals soften the envelopes surrounding the play and the actor, and permeable associations begin to develop. The process of preparing the incubation image alters the placement of the boundary. It is no longer between the actor and the play or character. Developing the incubation image places the actor, the character, and the world of the play in the same sphere. In lieu of separate envelopes, it puts in place a lively, networked matrix of questions *asked by the actor* of the play and the character in the form of the incubation image (or incubation body). The answers come in the form of the character's dreams expressed in the vernacular of the actor.[1]

The incubation image belongs to the actor, and the dreams belong to the character. Pay attention to the relationship between the two, the similarities of themes and actions. The network of questions the actor has about the character is embodied in the incubation image. Precise answers are yielded up in the dream because the incubation image acts like a magnet, attracting affinities to it out of the vastness of imagination. The dream is the raw material of the character's voice—the character's dream—out of which you evolve his dreamworked body. This dreamworked body is the compressed, elec-

---

1. The first example: the three-inch-long bound feet borne with pain and pride. Linda's vernacular symbolism became Nina's life.

trified expression of the character in dynamic relationship with the landscape of the play. The actor evokes it for a few moments prior to going out onstage, because within it resides the entire network of the stories upon stories, and psyches upon psyches, all unresolved, hungry, and alive. And the actor, feeling full and replete with living information, relaxes and lets it emerge as it will.

If this has been a cookbook of dreamwork, then time has arrived for specific recipes, the "How To's." Although there has been ongoing commentary throughout the incubations and dreamwork thus far, let's step back and analyze the specifics of two new incubations and dreams. I will interpolate many rules as we go so that theater people can conduct their own dreamwork. Smart theater people are talented and natively perceptive. They already intuit how to do this work. But there is nothing amiss when a natural born cook cracks open a book by Julia Child or Marcella Hazan to acquire some new cooking skills. So I lay out some measurements and ingredients for theater people to follow in learning to prepare the character's body. Your best guide in proceeding follows.

Believe that if you work patiently and slowly, paying careful attention to the actor's and the character's journeys, you will not go wrong.

Robert and I traveled to Los Angeles to work with ten people, teachers and professional acting students at the Ruskin School. Our object was to see what would happen when we developed work with actors who are naïve subjects with neither knowledge nor expectations of the technique or of us. John Ruskin is one of the premier teachers of Sanford Meisner's methods in the United States. As I am familiar with Meisner's work and John's reputation I knew we would find actors who met certain crucial requirements. They would honor the spontaneity of the unfolding action as they encountered it fresh in each exploration of the scene. And they would know what the scenes were about. In other words, they would strive from a simultaneous understanding of what is important to a scene without sacrificing the impulse for newly generated action and activity.

John and I worked out a few details two months before Robert and I arrived in Los Angeles. Ten actors would prepare five scenes from as few plays as possible. We ended up with three plays of John's choosing: two scenes from Steinbeck's *Of Mice and Men*, two from Anderson's *I Never Sang for My Father*, and one from Rabe's *Those the River Keeps*. The only restrictions I placed on the material were that it be well written and have some depth. The dreamwork works best with material that has heft. If what is required is the performance of light, surface behavior then the dreamwork is not a good match for the material. Because it creates dynamic associations between the actor, the character, and the world of the play it could freight too much subtlety or depth on something as undimensional as a sitcom scene, for example. I sent John a brief description (one paragraph each) of the incubation process, how to recall dreams, and the second step of the dreamwork process. He disseminated this information to the actors.

Preparing the incubation images over the phone began as a necessity, but by now has become our common practice. It is surprisingly easy to fall into an empathic work relationship over the phone, even with people you do not know. The readiest explanation as to why it works is that the dreamworker enters into the world of the actor, explicitly following the actor's cues, fleshing out the actor's vision. Everyone relaxes when his or her world is acknowledged as important and, moreover, expanded upon. It is a validating experience, and one that is easy to relax into.

Since I was writing, which required observing, Robert prepared the incubations. Each actor had a taped phone appointment. After some preparatory explanation, he asked them to describe the scene as it unfolded in their imaginations, not in the way it appeared on stage in rehearsal. Most people found this a relatively easy adjustment, but quickly clarified their momentary confusion by asking questions like, "You mean what I see now, or in rehearsal?" Robert asked which moment they wanted to incubate, and they were off and running.

Each incubation session lasts no longer than twenty minutes.

Unlike me, Robert exclusively treats the incubation material as he would dreams. He does not read the play in advance. He listens to what the actor says about the scene and which moment he wants to incubate and appraises the pathway they travel together as if the whole were a dream. That leaves selectivity—which images to choose and inhabit and from which to compose the incubation image—to Robert's astonishing understanding of the human psyche or, as he would say, human psyches. But I, with only the healthily developed sensitivity of a theater person and not a psychoanalyst, like to know the play. It clarifies the issues for me and to a degree affects my selectivity. However, and I must stress this, it does not do so in significant measure. The proper work in preparing the incubation image is to hear what the actor says about the scene, which moment is most troubling (or confusing or interesting, etc.) and then to follow the actor's vision. Letting the play guide me would be too controlling—too directorial.[2] This is true with one caveat: if I feel the actor fails to attend to a *crucial* element in the play I find a way to raise it in the flow of context. Robert, on the other hand, exquisitely stumbles

---

2. How are these functions different? As a director I follow the underlying narrative and play. The actor and I play detective to find ways to articulate it in action and activity. But to be frank, I do not accept an actor doing violence to what I believe the major line through is. In the dreamwork you are following the actor into character, and it is her journey—not the journey an audience will ultimately follow—that you must mine.

upon the necessary elements simply because he unearths them in his pursuit of the inner being of the actor as character. A case in point: in preparing Daniel Passer's incubation image from the Rabe play, *Those the River Keeps,* Daniel speaks about the life-and-death stakes that the character, Phil, experiences when he pleads with his wife to stay with him. Daniel recounts the scene and the moment he wants to incubate in this way:

> It is toward the end of the play. Susie has left Phil. She wants a baby, and in the past he has said he did not want one. She is looking to leave him permanently. He is trying to convince her that he has changed and does want a baby. By the end of the scene she does believe him. The section [to incubate is] where he drops to his knees and literally begs her to say. He says it is his soul talking, that he will crawl to her if that is what she needs. This is the part of the scene that most strikes me.

Daniel and Robert work for several minutes before Daniel reveals casually, "I [the character of Phil] am an aspiring actor. Before that I was a mafia hit man." Unfazed, and with a mild "Oh?", Robert incorporated this little time bomb into the incubation. I, on the other hand, would have known from reading the play that Phil was a former hit man struggling to stay out of that life after having paid dearly for leaving it. Robert teased out the unfolding information, honoring the assumption that what the actor said was wholly true. I would have been in possession of that nugget in advance. The results would be identical in any case, but I recommend that theater people read the plays in advance of preparing incubations.

One must find a place of inner balance about applying the narrative information judiciously. You want to respect what the actor says and follow his lead. It does not hurt to know the narrative of the play, but one cannot be imprisoned by it. At its heart the reason the dreamwork functions as it does is precisely because it operates as if the story of the play is a meta-story, underneath which lie dozens of connecting stories, each as important and as noisy as the meta-story. And each of these stories is operating simultaneously *and* being affected by the input of other stories while also affecting others with its output—giant feedback loops of storytelling, worldview, atmosphere, emotional states, and so on. Further, the dreamwork operates in both practice and theory on the principle that there are many psyches at work—different body-worlds within the same character—each with its own story, wrangling with one another, complementing one another, aware or ignorant of one another, conflicted by one another, and entirely indifferent to the existence of one another. The complexity and dynamism of the *real* story, difficult to express in words (see Proust or Henry James), demand that we honor them by not becoming prisoners of the meta-story. So we collapse out the narrative both when we prepare incubation images and when we work on dreams. We destroy it because we must destroy its tyranny to realize its true depths. We replace it with a network of impulses in the body. This network of impulses is what communicates with the autonomous imagination in dreaming.[3]

Let's look at the first part of the process, preparing an incubation image. Our ultimate goal is to collapse out the narrative to unearth the many stories that comprise it. We accomplish this in two steps. The first is to work as many elements of the unfolding scene as it is revealed by the actor's imagination during the session into the actor's body. You explore the images and couple them to embodied sensation and to any emotion that arises. The second is to build the

---

3. Another way to say this is that the plot is a result of the unfolding narrative. The actor's job is to reveal the underlying narrative(s) using the plot as guideposts. The plot should take care of itself if the actor has richly and fully embodied the narrative. Of course the dreamwork facilitates this precise task admirably.

incubation image, the seeded image representing the intersection between the actor and the character in relation to her world.

Here is a clear-cut example of this process. Jack Hannibal is an actor in Los Angeles who teaches at the Ruskin School.[4] He and Michael Laurie are acting a compilation of two scenes from *Of Mice and Men*. It uses sections of the first scene in the play in which George and Lenny's relationship and habitual behaviors are established. This is folded into the final scene of the play, when George kills Lenny.

Robert begins by asking Jack to describe the scene and to locate the moment he wants to incubate.

What do you see? Tell the story in the present tense, please.

Jack tells him:

> The scene takes place in a thicket by water. I tell Lenny earlier that if he ever gets into trouble he should come here and I will find him. At this point in the play, Lenny has murdered a woman. I come here to find him. Men are out looking for Lenny to lynch him. I have taken a handgun and have left them because I know where he is. What touches me about the scene is George's compassion. I don't want Lenny to stand trial and I don't want him tortured by an angry mob and executed. I take the decision into my own hands. He needs to be put down, sort of like an old dog.
>
> I find him and I am trying to get his attention. He is like a little child. There is a story he always makes me tell him about the life we are going to lead in the future. About how guys who work on ranches are the loneliest guys in the world because they have no families. They make money and blow it on liquor or at a cathouse. But we are not like this because we have each other and care about each other.

---

4. Subsequent to doing this work Jack opened his own acting studio in L.A.

And we are going to get a house one day. Lenny is so excited because at that house he will have a rabbit hutch and he can take care of the rabbits. When I find him he makes me tell him this story again. We go through it together. At the end I tell him to sit down and take his hat off. "I am going to tell it so you can see it. Take your hat off and look out across the river, because that is where you'll see it." That's where I back away from him as he starts to see the house and then I shoot him. I find it very touching.

Once you have a basic understanding of the scene, remind yourself of the moment to be incubated. You will often use it as the end point, but let it guide the journey. Start from an earlier part of the scene in order to work all elements into the body, and conclude with the "most confusing or interesting" moment.

Never *begin* with the most interesting or confusing moment. At the least, it is charged with emotion and therefore not a safe place to enter the scene. At most, it is the actor's question to her imagination, and all roads in the scene lead to or from that moment for the actor. You must work earlier elements into the body before hitting this high point in order to pose a carefully pressurized question to the autonomous imagination in dreams.

Jack Hannibal's sketch of the scene offers Robert a wide range of choices. Robert thought for a moment, sorting through the data, and said, "So the scene we should probably work is the moment when you are telling him about the house and you start to back off in preparation for shooting him." Why did he chose that moment rather than the actual shooting? Because the lead-up to pulling the trigger is the event most densely charged with emotion. The moment of the shooting is decisive; all choices are made, all emotions, however chaotic, get spent. And of course, it is anti-climactic.

If the moment an actor chooses to incubate contains an explosive or decisive release, incubate the lead-up, not the event itself.

Robert asks Jack:

Describe where you are as fully as you can. You say it is by a river?

Use leading phrases or statements to guide the actor into his own vision. While you never intrude your own opinion, you must often help the actor find his feet in the imaginary landscape. A question like, "You say it is by a river?" simply gives Jack a starting place.

Jack continues:

Yes. It is the 1930s and it is very hot. Steinbeck . . .

Guide the actor quickly and effortlessly away from the stage reality or the scripted reality and into his imagination. This is easy to do, but you must be firm and concise. Then immediately bring him into the physical reality of his body in the landscape.

Let go of Steinbeck and go to Jack. It's hot you say, and humid? Dry?

It feels humid.

And as you feel that are you sweating?

Yeah!

Jack is surprised to find himself having an unexpected embodied sensation.

What are you wearing?

Coveralls. And work boots. We are carrying our packs. We are essentially homeless.

And where do you see Lenny?

I see him behind me in a thicket of brambles.

What does he look like?

He's really big, 6'5", 6'6". Because of his size—he's not fat—he's just really big. He's not particularly muscular or defined, but everything about him is like a big child.

Be confident that the actor will follow you when you ask him to make a jump, whether it is jumping to a new frame or jumping into a different body. Your confidence becomes the actor's confidence. Then ask the actor a simple question about the physical environment as your opening bid. This plants his feet on the ground of the landscape and he will "just" see what you ask of him.

Robert directs Jack's attention to a new frame. He immediately follows that with the tangibility of what Lenny is actually doing as Jack imagines it in this new frame. Robert requests a simple piece of grounding information.

Can you go to the scene we are going to look at? He is sitting, or standing?

I call him out of the brambles and make him sit down. He is very excited because he knows something has happened. I try to calm him down. He is sitting at my feet, and we are both next to the river.

What do you feel toward him?

I feel this great remorse and loneliness that I can't even explain to him what he has done or what I have to do.

Always go to the body. Remember that the goal is to create embodied images that form a network of impulses. Take the actor from his emotion to his body, his state to his body, or the metaphor to his body. Ask the actor to locate where in his body he most strongly has the experience. Ask him to describe what that experience is like. Reflect back the actor's own words and focus the inquiry. Then direct his attention to his body.

Jack's statement that he feels remorse and loneliness is certainly made more astute by the explanation "that I can't even explain to him what he has done or what I have to do." But we are not looking for astuteness. His rational perception is important, but not to the dreamwork. It is already inherent in everything he says so we can bypass it neatly. We leave rationality behind after the first telling of the scene. We move through sensation, images, metaphor, and emotion to create the incubation image. We do not reject it aloud; we simply redirect the focus to the body.

> Can you focus in on that remorse and loneliness? Can you locate it in your body? Where do you feel it most strongly?
>
> In my chest.

Ask the actor to focus on physical sensation and wait as the sensation develops. Be patient. It will. You can further develop sensation by offering the actor visual details that surround the image.

> Focus on that for a moment. Feel what happens in your chest. He is now sitting and you are now standing. Is that so?
>
> Yeah.
>
> How is the weight on your feet as you stand there feeling this loneliness and remorse?

How someone stands on the ground is revealing. Asking an actor
about his stance, about how he supports himself, contains the seeds
of coded information from the literal through the metaphorical. It
also helps the actor maintain his connection in the landscape by staying "grounded."

> It's even, and I feel quite anchored. There is a feeling of timelessness,
> even though I know we are being chased, guys are out looking for
> Lenny. I feel like I have time.
>
> You can feel that in the way your feet are anchored?
>
> Yes, in my feet and in the remorse and loneliness.
>
> So feel the anchoring in your feet and the remorse and loneliness in
> your chest. Now, where do you have the gun?
>
> I have it in the back of my pants.
>
> And he is sitting there? And you are backing away from him? Or, how
> are you moving away from him?
>
> I actually come close to him and help him see—to look out—and
> once his imagination is caught I—

**Slow it down! When the actor is deep into his story he may pick up
the pace and compress the events. You both could easily miss several important movements. Tell him you want to slow it down. To
help him comply, direct him to the first moment in the sequence
you want to explore. Then help him focus on his body.**

> Let's slow it down. Can you go to the moment you are helping him
> see? Can you focus on your eyes that help him see? What is happen-
> ing to your eyes as you help him see?

Robert knows that Jack and he were ramping up to the most compelling moment. He is certain that there was a rich load of ore to
mine. He wants to explore each element carefully, selecting for the
incubation body.

> There is a lot. I see him and this is as close to him as I can get to say
> goodbye.

**Inch up to a major transition. Bring the actor to the brink with-
out going over.**

> Stay with that for a moment and feel as close as you can get to saying
> goodbye. What does that feel like?
>
> It's sad.
>
> And how does that sadness live in your body?
>
> It's as if there are hands on my shoulders keeping me back from him.
> It's a surrendered feeling.

**Make sure the actor can reinhabit the embodied images you feel
you may use for the incubation image. Return to them periodically.
Review them as the precursor to a shift in scene or a jump into a
new character.**

> So feel your shoulders, the hands on your shoulders and the surren-
> der in the shoulders, and the feeling that you are as close to him as
> you can get. And the loneliness and remorse in your chest. And the
> timeless feeling in your feet. Now, can you go to the moment when
> you pull the gun, before you pull the trigger? What is that like in
> your hand? Is it in your right hand or your left hand?

My right hand.

What is that like in your right hand?

It is heavy, like a rock. And I can feel the finality of it. That this is
something that is going to change reality.

Asking vague questions, such as "What it is like?," with regard to
something as concrete as a body part is a fundamental principle of
the dreamwork. Questions like this lead the actor to metaphor or
simile. Poetic metaphor is dense, layered. It is impossible to come to
the end of what a rock means. Focusing patiently on the body will
allow metaphorical imagery to emerge. When it does, immediately
couple the metaphor to the body part (a hand like a rock) and mirror it back to the actor. If you think of "the hand like a rock" as a
node in the network of impulses, then taking the time to dwell on
that image and probing it slowly allows that node to communicate
with another node in the networked system. More embodied poetry
may emerge as a result, as you are about to see.

Can you feel that in your hand?

Hmmm.

That this hand is going to change reality?

Yes. It feels like death.

If you feel that you are arriving at the moment of greatest emotion,
complexity, or intensity you may want to extend the exploration to
adjacent parts of the body. More and more information may flow
forth.

Can you sense into that death that the hand will dispense and change
reality? How does that feel in your arm?

I feel like I am standing in my love for him and what we have been to each other. And it's like this gun is like a pair of scissors that will cut him free of it.

Now this experience of standing in your love for him and holding the scissors that will cut him free, what is that like in your body?

It is heavy.

Any place in particular where the heaviness is most concentrated?

Around my head. As if I had a concussion, where time and everything is wobbling.

It is clear that Robert had taken Jack to the point of George's greatest passion and compassion. Jack is next led through all the selected embodied images.

Generally incubate two-thirds of the embodied images from the actor's character's perspective and one-third from the other character's perspective. This is a loose estimate, but do include something from the other character. In plays, two characters (or more) affect each other's reality, and it is this composite reality, with all of its questions, that will be incubated.

Can you focus on that? Hold that. So feel with your head the wobbling. In your shoulders, being pushed down. The weight of the heavy rock in your hand. The chest that feels lonely and remorseful. The feet that are anchored and timeless. Can you feel that?

Yes.

Stay with that. Now focus on Lenny. Now, I want you to get into Lenny's ecstatic vision. How is he sitting?

He is on his knees and his hands are on his thighs. You can see the enchantment of his mind. He is ecstatic. You can see he is lost in the fantasy.

Can you sense into the way he is lost in this vision?

It is totally abandoned.

Feel his total abandon. What does this do to his sense of body?

It makes him electric.

Can you feel the electricity?

Yeah.

What does the electricity do?

It is bright, and makes me feel small. I know that this is the end of hope and possibility.

When the actor slips out of the element you wish him to explore, simply direct him back where you want him. Follow this by immediately bringing the actor into embodied sensation. Jack slipped out of Lenny's perspective and into George's.

That is not in Lenny's perspective. Try to stay in Lenny's perspective.

Lenny is just transported.

Feel this transportment. Is that the electric state?

Yes.

Sense how the electricity moves through his body in this state of transport. Now as you feel this electric transport can you also feel what is happening in the head, the shoulders, and the chest, and the feet? The heaviness in the hand? And at the same time also feel that electric transport. Really etch this in your physical memory. This is the incubation image.

Selection of specific images that comprise this network of impulses quickly becomes an intuitive process. There are a couple of organizing principles that should help when you begin. One method is to select at least three elements that express:

1. Something of the actor's character's contact with the environment

2. Something of the central action of the moment being incubated

3. Something of the other character.

Although it contained more than three images, we could analyze Jack Hannibal's incubation image into the three categories.

1. Contact with the environment: the feet that are anchored and timeless; the chest that feels lonely and remorseful.

2. Contact with the event: the wobbling in your head; your shoulders being pushed down; the weight of the heavy rock in your hand.

3. The other character: Lenny's electric transport.

Developing the incubation image is easier done than said. Let's think it through for a moment. The actor tells his story, and despite the fact that we are collapsing the narrative into a network of impulses, he remains influenced by the meta-narrative. You, as the dreamworker, know which moment he wants to incubate: this is the incubation event. You begin earlier than the incubation event to create the landscape in which it takes place. The logic to starting earlier is that if multidimensional cause and effect creates the event then you must incubate the underlying stories that generate it. But instead of selecting storytelling images exclusively about the play's plot and narrative, you create a network, points on a woven, dimensional pattern, each of which is telling its own story about the story. You trust that tenacious imaginative tendrils connect the actor to the event he is incubating.[5] You fill out the landscape prior to its occurrence and then move to the event itself. You close with the other character's perspective at the time of the event, although this could be introduced earlier in the flow.

There are other guiding principles to selecting the embodied images that comprise an incubation image. One is to choose images that represent oppositions or simple contrasts; another is to incubate transitional states. But I will describe them in detail during the next actor's incubation.

Jack Hannibal's incubation produced an exquisite dream and fluid, unconstrained acting. But first the dream. I will annotate the rules of the process as we go.

When Robert and I arrived in Los Angeles, Jack told us about his incubated dreams.

> I had two really pronounced dreams. I am in Utah with my friend, Rima, and there is a guy with us. We are on this hill and there is a wild, huge, golden field and the sun is setting. There is a herd of buffalo, black, monstrous. We get really close to them. There is something that is so beautiful, so awesome that I scream—"Rrrawow!"— and the buffalo stampede. The three of us run. We jump a split rail fence. We are in the street—a dirt road in the middle of nowhere. This guy with us is terrified, but so excited. We are all really alive. Rima knows me, so she knows that this is something that I would do, so it is not such an issue.
>
> Then I am in line in a really quaint, very chi-chi restaurant. Low ceilings, exposed beams. I am in line to pay. This guy who's been with

---

5. And you should trust it. A human being's consumption and retention of stories are guaranteed. And an actor's preservation of the play's plot is the safest bet. What actor doesn't know what *happens* in a play?

us is standing in front of me. This very large guy who is his boss asks him why he is not wearing his uniform. The guy has no answer for him. The atmosphere turns grave. It is not casual that the guy has forgotten it. The big guy is kind of pompous but he is really earthbound. There is a serenity about him; he's like the buffalo. He asks the guy if he is drunk. The guy kind of smiles and I know right there that he has lost his job. I don't like this restaurant or chi-chi places, yet there is something about the boss—what he radiates—that makes it seem very appropriate that he wants his business conducted completely anonymously, with absolute discipline, and you feel that it makes sense. He doesn't raise his voice. He doesn't do anything. He just steps away from the group of us. He gets on his cell phone—he is either reporting to someone higher up or making arrangements to have a new assistant.

The people I have been in line with are all sitting in rows. Either I have just acted something—there is a white sheet on the floor that I am folding—it could be something I have written and directed, or something I am performing. And my sister is there talking to these people, telling them about me and what they have just seen. And I know that I am about to get an important job. And I know that whoever these people are, they are very powerful.

And I am with one of them, a woman, very attractive, and I am going into her bedroom, which is my mother's bedroom in the house I grew up in. And the room is very dark, but the closet door by the window is open (there is a big bed and a fireplace with no fire in it), and there is a light coming from inside the closet.

I had one other dream. I am in my parents' house in East Hampton and I go out back. There are these rolling fields and I am out there exploring. The grass is very high. There are long, wooden sheds. As I walk through the grass I am walking through people's skeletons. I am walking through their ribs and their spines, smashing them and turning them to dust. I am stuck in this grassy graveyard. The sheds are a concentration camp. I make my way through the bodies and I get to a

kind of hill behind these sheds. There is a railroad track stretching
across this great plain. And right next to it is this high stack of bodies
that runs next to the track all the way. It is horrifying. I turn around. I
recognize two new dirt roads that have been put in. Two cars are driving—I *never* see cars—I realize that this place that I am in is going to
be developed; it is too valuable. And no one will remember what happened here. I go to get out of there. I come to this gigantic ranch that
is under construction. The bottom of it is glass and steel girders. It is
massive. On top of it is a deck that surveys the whole land, with lawn
chairs and a couple of umbrellas. I have been here before. I pull open
the glass doors and walk inside. Nicole Rosseli's father is there, sweeping. I feel so glad to see him because he is the guy who caught me there
the last time I cut through this place. He was very kind about it. I
know he is the owner. I am so grateful to see another human being. But
the moment I get up to him he pulls out a suede jacket with hanging
tassels. He tells me that he will sell it to me for half off and this is not
so much a ranch as a warehouse for the manufacturing of these coats.
As he is going on about what a great deal he'll give me I get really
scared and dizzy. I start thinking about the bodies in the back and I
know that the animals that go into making these coats are the people. I
don't know what to say to this guy. And I get dizzier. And then John
[Ruskin] is there with Stacy [Gordin] and he grabs the coat out of the
guy's hand and haggles over the price. He runs around asking questions
about construction and the operation of the warehouse. He is going to
buy the coat. He decides to invest in the company because it is a huge
worldwide thing. I get violently ill, and I think I am going to be vomit.
And I go outside and see my parents' house. It is the last place on earth
I want to go. But I am so overwhelmed and I so badly need shelter that
I just walk toward the house.

These are lengthy dreams with a great deal of material. How do
we choose what to explore when there is so much data?

Allow the dreams to affect you. Which moments moved you? Which seemed less interesting? Which had symbolic qualities? Answering these questions one could easily dismiss the restaurant manager in the first dream in favor of the feet crushing the skeletons in the second dream. Like cream rising to the surface, the stampeding buffalo, the concentration camp, and the suede jacket made of human skin all float, demanding to be recalled. All three of these images comply with another rule.

If given a variety of images, choose the ones with the strongest imaginative qualities, those that relate least to the actor's everyday life. Jack's daily existence is comprised of restaurants and auditions, so we can let these pass in favor of the sheer imagination of the stampeding buffalo and the concentration camp skeletons.[6]

Choose correlating images within the dreams. The images may correlate one for one or they may simply allude to one another. In these dreams they are the herd of buffalo, the suede jacket made of human skin and the skeletons lying on the ground.

Choose actions in the dreams that are reminiscent of—or explicitly like—the scene or to the incubation image.

Choose character elements common to the incubation image, the play, and the scene.

The dumb wisdom of the buffalo magnificently symbolizes George's feelings about Lenny. Lenny lost control and killed Curly's

---

6. On the other hand, I once had a friend to whom I told an apocalyptic dream I'd had the night before. He looked at me, perplexed, and said, "Last night I dreamt I went to the store and bought a loaf of bread." He was not joking. But be assured that we'd find a gold mine in the loaf of bread once we entered the landscape.

Wife, and the frightened buffalo in the dream stampede. The symbolism of animals out of control is also echoed in the men who hunt Lenny. George knows that if they catch Lenny their violence could exceed all bounds. And certainly we, as Americans, walk with internalized images of the Native American buffalo hunt and the animals' wholesale extinction. Killing Lenny is merciful, but George knows it represents the extinction of innocence and the end of value in his own life. Parallels to these are found throughout the dreams from the inhumanity of the concentration camp executions to the nauseating devaluation of human life by turning it into a skin jacket.

And finally, remember the moment the actor incubated. Jack incubated the moment when George kills Lenny. What interested him was how touching it was. What images in the two dreams evoke compassion? As I listened to Jack's dreams, they were the primordial dumb wisdom of the buffalo, the horror of the concentration camp skeletons, and Jack's aversion to the jacket made from human skins. In George's fatal act, horror and compassion are mixed in the same state.

Limit your walk through the dream landscape to twenty minutes. Choose an opening image and begin. Do not be afraid.

I suspect that the manager of the restaurant had as much to say about the *Of Mice and Men* scene as anything else in the dreams. So if you miss an image that I might think is important, you are probably mining an important image I might have skipped. Both could be equally valid for the actor, the character, and the world of the play.[7] Screwing your courage to the sticking place, you must enter the

---

7. A good example of this comes up in the work of Sharon Repass, which is next.

dream landscape. This is always a slightly apprehensive moment for everyone, irrespective of experience. Take heart and start walking slowly. No one knows the unknown any better than anyone else.

Choose a moment of comparative safety in which to enter the dream landscape. Or, choose a benign dream character with whom to enter. This creates a feeling of safety for both the actor and you. Anchor the image and sensation well so the actor can return to it. The safe place—or person—is a haven to retreat to if the dreamwork gets too intense.

Robert begins,

> Can you go to the moment when you stand in front of the closet in your mother's room? Can you describe what you see?

At the end of the concentration camp dream Jack explicitly refers to his parents' house as a place of shelter, despite it being the last place on earth he wants to be. Shelter is a good indicator that there is safety to be found there. In an earlier dream scene he discovered light and familiarity in his mother's room, making it a safe place to begin. But a moment of comparative safety may not be as plainly marked. Use your sense. When you listened to the dreams there were safe, if uneventful places where the sun shone, the air was pleasant, things were homey or familiar. Or perhaps there were characters who were supportive and understanding, even if they were adjunct to the incubated event.[8] Go there, putting the actor into that landscape. If the safe place is a person, go to the person. Tease out what she looks like, where she is in the landscape, what her effect is on the actor, and where it can be found in his body. Then move on from there.

---

8. Anthony Arkin re-entered his dream with his wife, Amelia.

Jack continues.

Yeah, there are all these colors there. All these clothes. It is warm,
there is a window. And a blue sky out the window.

Can you see the closet itself?

Yes.

Is it open?

Yes.

Is there a difference between the light inside the closet and outside
the closet?

Lighting is atmospheric and conveys subtle clues to the actor.
Explore the quality of the light. In life we are bathed in light at all
times. Our dreams often match the pattern of the light of an autobiographical experience, with the light in the dream experience yielding
up symbolic emotional states replete with autobiographical stories.

If there is a contrast, it is always a good idea to feel through it.
In this case Robert explores the light in the closet with the contrast
of the darkness of the room. Oftentimes unexpected riches that are
important to network reside in the contrast.

Yes, in the bedroom itself it is dark. The only light is natural light; it
is late afternoon, early evening. It is that awful twilight. The shades
are down. And there is a very oppressive darkness.

Can you sense into the oppression of it? What happens in your body
with the oppression of your mother's bedroom?

**When the actor reveals a strong embodied sensation, always ask
him to focus on it for a moment.** You may end up using it as a part

of the dreamworked body, or you may let it pass. In either case it will bring the actor further into the present of the imaginary landscape, which is where you want him.

It's like I can't get a full breath of air.

Pursue any image in the dream that suggests that the actor is entering from one world into another. Robert entered the dream landscape through the safe place of the closet, but he used it as a part of the dreamworked body for a different reason. I feel honor bound to report this to the reader, but I have to admit that if I were doing the dreamwork with Jack I might have missed it. But learning what to look for is the purpose of this chapter. Robert's reasoning for selecting the closet is that when Jack enters the mother's room a transitional world reveals itself. On one side are safety, colors, and warm light. On the other are darkness, oppression, and bated breath. Robert used the mother's room to open to another world, the world of stampeding buffalo and the world of concentration camp victims and horror. Jack's thematic rendering of the Steinbeck text revealed to Robert that George cannot kill Lenny until he believes that Lenny has entered "another world," the safe place of the rabbits. At that point the gun is no longer a weapon of destruction, but it becomes a transportation device taking Lenny to that better place and away from present horror. It's a beautiful movement. The same issue arises more clearly in the next scene in this chapter, so we can revisit it as a rule at that time.

Stay with that for a moment please. Describe the difference of the light inside the closet.

It's the exact opposite. Very bright, rich, warm.

Can you sense into the rich warmness of the light in the closet? What is it like in the body, this rich warmness of the closet?

It's like I have wings. It's like my back is opening up.

Stay with that. As you feel your back opening up can you also feel your lungs that cannot breathe in the darkness?

Yes.

Robert has now created the safe place and has mined the transitional world. He shifts the scene.

Now can you go to the first moment when you see the buffalo?

This great, big, black face. Huge. So ancient. Dumb.

Can you sense what happens to you when you see this ancient, dumb face?

I just want to hug it, grab it.

Feel that.

Robert knows, along with everyone else in the room, that he has struck gold. You can simply feel it. He makes sure to expand this image of the buffalo-as-Lenny so that it infuses Jack's body. When it is anchored, he will move on to the stampede.

Can you see its body?

Uh huh. It is huge. They have these narrow hips—it's funny.

As you look at this huge, dumb face can you sense what kind of atmosphere comes from that face—what kind of sense is in that face?

It's like the greatest wisdom.

Can you sense into that dumb wisdom? What is it like to be in this archaic, dumb wisdom?

Simple.

Can you feel inside the body of this archaic, dumb wisdom—this huge body with the narrow hips?

Yeah.

Can you feel the moment when the stampede begins?

Yeah, it's just this great power coming up that—

Slow it down. What is it like, this great power coming up?

There is no thought in it. The energy is coming right up out of the earth.

Feel that. What is it like for that force to start a stampede?

It's awesome. It is elemental.

Can you feel the elemental force? What is like that?

My heart is ripping open.

When an image is a full as it can be, move on. Recognizing this moment does take some experience, but it is pretty obvious. The power of a heart that is ripping open, stampeded by dumb wisdom is enormous. It is an image filled with unspent action, its potential still intact. Robert moves on to the next images in the dreams.

Stay with that. Keep feeling that. Stay in your heart feeling the power of this stampede of dumb wisdom coming into your body. As you feel that can you see the moment when you first step on the dead bodies? What is the sound?

It's like old sticks, dried wood.

If the imagery suggests that an odor might be present, or perhaps a sound, ask for it. If none reveals itself simply move on. Smell is the oldest of our senses, and some say that hearing came next in our development. If you can locate an odor it may open onto a primitive state that would immediately deepen the experience while bypassing the intellect.

Smell?

Dust. Death.

Can you sense into that death? What is it like to be stepping into so much death?

It's that same wisdom.

Jack cries and does not stop for a long while.

Tears are not a measure of success in this process. In fact, they are at cross-purposes to doing the work. The crying actor has to be guided back to the landscape. The tears are *not* the work; embodying the imagery is. Although Jack is deeply moved, Robert presses on after a respectful pause. Jack stays with Robert and his sobbing subsides, although he cries gently for a while. Robert prompts Jack back to the work with, "When you have a free moment," meaning, "Make room for the inner impulse to work and tell me what happens in your body."

If the crying continues unabated, remind the actor to stay with the image. If that fails, you can take the actor back to the anchored safe place. Then either ask the actor to look at the upsetting imagery from the perspective of the safe place or integrate the safe place into the incubation image or the dreamworked body. The actor requires that perspective to balance himself.

Robert continues.

Stay with it. Now look at the piles and piles of bodies along the track. Now see the coat made of those bodies. Stay with it. What happens in your body? When you have a free moment and you can speak tell us what happens in your body.

My heart pours right into that wisdom.

Keep on feeling it.

And I know that I am of the same. And that my awareness of being outside of it and having a separate life is irrelevant.

What is it like in your body, that sense?

It is a surrender. A letting go. Everything feels open.

Stay with that sense of the openness and that nothing matters.

I just want to rage.

Feel that rage. Just feel it. As you feel the rage feel the stampede. As you hear the stampede hear the sound of stepping on the dry stick bones. And the smell of dust. Can you feel all of that?

Yeah.

Buffalo, innocence, archaic wisdom, death, bones, murder, ripping heart: This is a big dream with powerfully disturbing images. But then, George has to kill Lenny, which is powerfully disturbing to the character and the actor. Jack had a lot to handle, but he is handling it. He is staying with Robert and working. Robert intends to buoy these images by taking Jack back to the safe place. As you will see, the result of returning to the safe place is not necessarily hearts and flowers. All of the disturbing images are shored up by the safe place, but it is not a pretty picture.

Now, look into the closet and see the light. What are you feeling?

I just want to tear this closet apart. I want to knock off the side of
this house. This light is so puny and fake. And yet I am desperate for
it.

How does it feel in your body, this desperation for the puny, fake
light?

Everything is closing, my chest, my throat is closing, my stomach is
in a knot.

As I said before, a knotted stomach, an exploding heart, the inability
to breathe indicate fully potentiated imagery to the dreamworker. This
particular movement has reached an end point. The node in the network is explored. The actor has gone from image to sensation to
metaphor and then to an expanded embodied sensation. All of these
are expressed (and alive and firing) in the knotted stomach.

Contrariwise, some roads you pursue don't seem to take you anywhere picturesque. Explore and embody—and when it doesn't reveal
much of anything, simply move on. You only have twenty minutes.

Robert continues:

Feel the knot in your stomach. Now, from the knot in your stomach
can you look at the dumb face of the buffalo? Can you feel the power
of that force? Can you feel it go on a stampede?

Yeah.

Jack wept but advances every step of the way with Robert.

Can you feel it at the same time as the knot in your stomach? Can
you feel it in your heart? And the sound of the sticks. And the coat
that is made of the dead bodies. And the wobble in the head? Can
you feel all of that?

Hold the images that make up the dreamworked body together for a full minute before ending the process. Check in with the actor to make certain he can feel them and see them.

Stay with it. Stay in it. Stay in it.

How did Robert choose these images? As I mentioned earlier, Robert recalled Jack saying that George is able to pull the trigger once Lenny is safely out of danger in the world of the rabbits. From the perspective of the knot in the stomach, which you could view as George standing at a doorway gazing out to another world, he looked out on the dumb, archaic wisdom on the buffalo. And because this state of gazing out into another world was as essential to George for Lenny's sake as for his own, Robert chose to explore these images as parts of the incubation body. Always scout out the thematic or sensate affinities among the play, the incubation, and the dreams.

We can also apply the same selection criteria to these dream images that we used to prepare the incubation image. They were contact with the environment, contact with the event, and contact with the other. In the incubation image the actor was in contact with these objects. In the dreamworked body, we shift emphasis to the character in contact with these objects.

- The character in contact with the environment: the knot in the stomach; the feeling in the heart; the sound of the sticks.

- The character in contact with the event: the concussive, wobbling head (this image contained inside of it the hand like a rock, like death); the coat made of skins; the feeling of the stampede.

- The character in contact with the other: the dumb archaic wisdom in the face of the buffalo.

When Michael and Jack played the scene after we'd dreamworked Jack's body it was wholly altered for them both. Most striking to me, internal rhythms were born of discernible, although not intellectually identifiable, specificity. Internal referents connected every word. George was inexpressibly loving, a state that was simultaneously comprised of annoyance, frustration, fear, tenderness, hopelessness, and need. Lenny was blissfully lost in his vision—transported. In the embrace of George's forgiveness and love he entered the beautiful world of rabbits, his heart's desire. George, emotionally full to bursting, had a terrible, compassionate, violent task to do, and this action was the vessel that contained his turmoil. The scene was replete with their relationship and at the same time with the horrible pressure of George finding the way to act on his decision. The audience was excruciatingly aware in every moment that George faced an empty, sordid life without Lenny.

When I asked Jack about the process, from preparing the incubation body to dreamworking the character's body, he offered this response.

> The incubation seemed straightforward enough. When we entered the scene and found the defining moment, my perspective moved back and forth from being immediately inside the scenario to looking down at it from above. Each time Robert asked me to describe what I was feeling in a part of my body my consciousness moved there like a comet through Jello. Everything felt like it was in a semi-liquid state. Nothing was solid. When my attention arrived in my hand for instance, there would be a moment while the whole universe reformed and congealed in the wake of its movement. Once settled I was able to report quite clearly what sensations I was having.
>
> What I found so interesting about the dreamwork is the way it by-passed my intellect and steeped me in the deep, mysterious waters of this other source (call it what you will). After we worked on my

dreams and ran the scene a second time, I felt wholly alive in the circumstances and more emotionally connected than I'd been the first time through, but I didn't really know why. It was as if my mind had been overwhelmed from below by something so powerful that it couldn't even begin to process what was happening, couldn't comprehend it. Though this was a new experience and a little unsettling due to the unfamiliarity, I loved it. What a vacation it was from the run-of-the-mill tedium of my mind. In the days following the workshop I could feel my conscious mind slowly regaining dominance over the wellspring the workshop had tapped into. This came in the form of insights and understanding about the dreamwork and its relation to the scene I did. Bit by bit my mind put the experience into a context it could comprehend and thus control. I would have liked the opportunity to see how it held up over time. I wonder if the power of what was tapped into could be sustained over time (say the run of a play) or would it become less potent as the mind had a chance to corral the experience with understanding.

Several actors talked to me about the unusual intimacy the group experienced as they watched each other work with their dreams, reminiscent of what happened to the group of younger actors when they prepared themselves to dream for *The Illusion*. In retrospect, Jack Hannibal felt that the dreamwork process required a closing movement that returned the actors to the everyday world. He felt "not quite [him]self," in the days that followed. As this was the first time we'd worked with a group of actors with whom we did not share a prior relationship, I'll consider his suggestion seriously for the future.

I do not share the curiosity inherent in Jack's comment about wanting to see if the effects of the dreamwork held up over time. I am not concerned about an actor's conscious consumption of the imaginative artifacts of the dreams. I don't think that is likely if the actor were making the whole play. Any actor doing ongoing work on a role knows how to protect her sources. She would not allow herself to analytically "use up" her dreamworked body. If Jack had returned to a rehearsal of *Of Mice and Men* on the following day, his actor's instincts would have been as protective. What does intrigue me is the other aspect of Jack's question. Could the high standard of both process and performance set when actors dreamwork their bodies be sustained? Using dreamwork repeatedly as a method with an ensemble dedicated to that level of work is the next logical step. It will be interesting to see the outcome.

The more difficult problem to address relates to how an individual actor employs dreamworking if no one else in the cast or company joins the process. Would it skew the landscape if one actor let herself live inside a networked character's body without the other actors breathing the same air? It is a real possibility. Developing the incubation image offers excellent research, but the dreamworked body might derail the consensual ensemble.

The next set of dreamwork also comes from *Of Mice and Men*. I chose it because Sharon Repass, the actor playing Curly's Wife, asked to incubate something exclusively from the character's memory—an event not found in the text except as a glancing reference. This piece also gives us a chance to juxtapose working on images sequentially (as Robert did with Jack) with working on simultaneously by holding together transitional states. Transitional states are a more complex movement, but a powerful medium in the process. But I run ahead of myself. The final reason to use this particular scene is that it crosses into explicitly sexual material whose proper negotiation requires a good, working example.

This incubation was wild and impressive. Sharon was alone with her four-month-old baby and her needy dog, Rosebud. Interruptions were clearly going to be the norm. Robert surprised me by saying, "Don't worry about interruptions. The work we are about to do can be easily interrupted without harm." This was news to me, so I lis-

tened with added curiosity. To this point the only constant we had
was focused concentration. Robert's suggestion that Sharon should
not be troubled by a bumpy process replete with guaranteed interruptions was a wonderful hypnotic postulate. In other words, "There
is no way to fail at this, even in disturbed and distracted conditions.
It's easy." Sharon relaxed far more deeply than I thought possible for
a mother alone with a four-month-old, and the results were fascinat-
ing. Every time she returned from comforting the baby or the dog or
both simultaneously, she immediately dropped right back into a
working state. This concentration spoke highly of her skill.

Curly's Wife, the only woman in the play and the only character
with no name, is a masterpiece of playwriting technique. Feeling desperately isolated on the ranch, she knows she has made a recent, bad
marriage. Curly is an abusive, jealous husband who crowds her and
would constrain all of her movements if he could. Or perhaps Curly
wouldn't be as bad an egg as he clearly is if she quit wandering out of
their home and over to the ranch hands. Does his tyranny drive her
out of their home, or do her needs make her seek out the company
of other men, or both? Curly's Wife needs to be admired and recognized. I have seen productions in which she is played as a promiscu-
ous slut, but Steinbeck leaves it to the actor to flesh out what the
character knows of herself and acts upon, and what she does not
know about herself that influences her behavior. These decisions
frame what the audience feels about her. Steinbeck gives Curly's Wife
a spare but surprisingly evocative background. The choices about how
that background shaped her are very much the actor's and director's.

Sharon is a smart actor. She chose to incubate the moment when
Curly's Wife describes a childhood event to Lenny. At root, it will
address questions about her character's behavior, specifically about
sexual matters. They meet in the barn while the men play horseshoes
outside. She sneaks in her suitcase and plans to bolt when the ranch
quiets into night. Lenny sits on the floor of the barn, burying and

uncovering his dead puppy that he accidentally killed in play. He
worries about what George will say. Lenny and Curly's Wife speak,
side by side, about their individual concerns, but ultimately they find
each other soothing. She affectionately calls him a big baby and
understands why he likes to touch pretty, soft things. She offers to let
Lenny touch her hair, and within moments of doing so Lenny loses
control of himself. When she struggles to stop him, he kills her.
Sharon says of the moment she wants to incubate,

> Her mother and father had awful fights when she was a child, and
> one night during one of these the father came into her room and
> took her way. He tells her—it is pretty much a fantasy—that in their
> new life alone together there won't be any more arguments, there
> would be pretty, baked cakes, and pictures painted on the walls. In
> the morning they caught us and took him away. Soon after that he
> died. "In the morning they caught us" is ambiguous. Did he molest
> her? I feel that he did.

Robert begins to unearth the state between Curly's Wife and Lenny
in the barn that enables her recall of this memory to unfold. Very
soon Sharon and Robert will exit the barn and go into memory alone.

> Can you tell me where you are with Lenny?
>
> I am in a barn area. It's dark. There is a lot of hay. It's cold. There is
> a little light coming through the cracks.
>
> So you are sitting in a kind of semi-darkness. How far away is Lenny
> from you?
>
> I am pretty close to him.
>
> What of him do you see?
>
> I see him out of my peripheral vision.

But your concentration is elsewhere?

Yes.

Can you tell me about the focus you are having? What are you remembering?

I am remembering what it was like with my dad. He was a lot of fun. He got drunk a lot, but I loved him. He was an artist.

How old are you in this memory?

It's funny. I'd say five, but I don't think it is accurate.

No, no, you are five. What do you remember of the story?

I remember my parents arguing . . .

When the actor stops generalizing, slow down the process and take her more deeply into detailed imagination. When Sharon said, "I am remembering what it was like with my dad. He was a lot of fun. He got drunk a lot, but I loved him. He was an artist," it had none of the tonal qualities of the action of remembering. Once Robert asked, "How old are you?" Sharon actually looked, and immediately conjoined the action: to remember. That is when Robert had to slow things down so they could enter by degrees into her vision.

Now, slow down there. What kind of arguing is going on?

They are screaming.

What does the screaming do to your five-year-old body?

It makes me scared.

What happens to your breathing?

I can't breathe.

Are you trying to hide?

Yes, under the covers. Huh. I feel scared.

What happens in your body as you feel scared like this?

I feel like I want to curl up in a ball.

Go to the curling up. Where in your body do you feel the beginning of the curling up?

My face.

What is happening in your face?

I feel like I want to go inside.

As you feel that, what is happening in your face?

It is getting all scrunched up.

How do you first become aware that your daddy has come to you?

I hear him.

What does that do to you?

I am scared at first.

Are you scared he is going to do something to you?

Yeah.

Notice that Robert refrains from pressing for an answer to this question. I will discuss this matter in greater depth at the end of Sharon's incubation, but for the moment, let us just say he refrained from prurience, although there were two other issues at play here as well.

How are his footsteps? Are they steady?

No, they are erratic.

So, he is drunk.

Yes.

And you know this as a kid?

Yes, I know it.

How does he enter the room?

He storms in.

What is your first reaction when he storms in?

I go under the covers.

Can you still feel it in your face?

Yes.

And then what happens?

He pulls the covers down and picks me up. He tells me he wants to leave.

What is your reaction when he picks you up? What is the first reaction as his body touches yours?

I am scared.

Where is the fear in your body?

In my head. I feel that curling up feeling still.

How does he hold you?

In a cradle.

Remember to investigate the other senses when they logically arise. Here is a clear cut example of a moment to ask about the sense of smell. Robert knows the father has been drinking and asks,

Can you smell?

Yes.

What does his alcohol smell like?

Awful. Dirty. He smells.

Don't forget to review powerful embodied images so that the actor can reinhabit them. Not only may you want to use them in the incubation body, but you are also collapsing out the narrative by networking the responses. Each of these responses continues firing (and storytelling) once embodied.

> OK, stay with that. So, the smell of alcohol and the feeling of wanting to curl up and the feeling in the head. Then he tells you that he wants to leave.

The smell of the alcohol and the feeling of wanting to curl up and the feeling in the head represent one pole.

> Yes, he is sick of this house and wants to take me with him.
>
> And what do you feel about that?
>
> I am kind of glad. He is calming down, I guess. He's making the idea of leaving exciting. I want to believe him.

The moment between states is highly charged with electricity and information. Sharon moves between fear of the stinking father and the desire to believe him. In one state the medium, the environment created by opposing forces, is stable. In the next state the medium is stable. But in between, as they struggle in opposition before eventually moving from one to another, exists a lively, unstable transitional medium. This in-between state contains all of the issues of the opposition, all of the hopes and fears, the conflicting desires, and the embodied responses.

Work slowly to incubate the in-between moment. This struggle between oppositions is a gold mine. You must proceed in increments.

- Explore the movement from the emotion to how it is expressed in the body.

- Explore where the body concentrates the physical sensation most forcefully.

- See if sensation resides anywhere else. Does a metaphor emerge?

- When you feel the image is pressurized, close the loop by reintroducing the initial stimuli as part of the node's name.

This pattern can emerge in different orders, but the principle remains the same. It is like plucking the strings of an instrument one at a time. They vibrate until they become a chord with sympathetic overtones resonating between the strings.

> Go to the point where you want to believe him. You don't believe him yet but you want to believe him.
>
> I don't like it there at home either.
>
> Do you have a sense that this is a fantasy?
>
> Yes, I do, but I want to believe him.

To mine the in-between state, you must categorically direct the actor toward the opposing poles. Sharon's last two responses may have filled in her ability to take these next steps, but they were useless as nodes in the network. The first was too informational, and the

second simply restated the desire. Robert has to direct Sharon back
to her desire and to keep her focused there until it is fully expressed
in her body.

> Go into the wanting to believe him, the desire that what he says be
> true. Stay with that. How does that desire that what daddy says is
> true live in your body?
> A longing.

> Feel the longing in your body. What part of your body is the longing
> concentrated in?

> My heart. There is a reaching out.

> Does it go through your arms?

> Yeah, my chest. It is strongest there.

> Stay with the longing in your chest. Keep feeling it there how you
> long for what daddy says to be true.

Sharon cries and Robert keeps her focused on her chest, not the tears.

> I want to hold him.

> OK, feel that.

This was an interesting moment that is hard to describe. "I want to
hold him" felt pallid in comparison to the longing in the chest. It
doesn't read that way on the page, however. But I cite it because
Robert acknowledged what Sharon said and moved back to exploring
the transitional state. It brings up a hard and fast rule.

Never reject a product of the actor's imagination. If you cannot use it well, acknowledge it and move on. The process will not be successful if there is violence, and the actor would experience a rejection of her imagination as violent. She would suddenly be wrong, and that would be the end of the work.

> As you want to hold him and you have the feeling in your chest, are you slowly starting to believe him?
>
> I am trying to. It's hard. He smells like alcohol. I am trying, I think I can.
>
> It's an effort. But I think I can do it.

Bingo! Sharon goes right to the struggle that exists between opposing forces in the in-between state (the fear of the stinking father and the desire to believe him). She calls it "effort," which can be embodied. Robert explicitly asks her,

> Can you feel the effort?
>
> Yes.
>
> Focus on where the effort is.
>
> Not breathing.
>
> Not breathing and also feel the longing in the chest.
>
> It's a real struggle.
>
> Stay with that struggle. Feel it a moment longer so it is anchored.

If you embody a state in one body part and then later the actor reports a new state in the same body part, develop the image a little further to see if you can place the new state in its own distinct physical location.

Exception: If these two states are part of an opposition and the actor reports that both are represented in the same body part, go with it. Be careful to name each distinctly. Hold them together to create the complex, dynamic in-between state.

Robert and Sharon walk further through the memory. He brings her from the bedroom, to the road, and finally to a cheap motel where the child and father spend the night. When Sharon says (below) that she is scared it has a present, expressive quality; she is not commenting or observing.

Yes. I am alone with him. At night. Not with mommy anymore.

Allow that fear to come in. Where are you going?

A motel. Oh, I am scared now.

They are about to approach the event that Sharon wants to incubate. Has the father molested her? She suspects so. She is loath to freight an untruth on the scene and the reference in the text is ambiguous. But Curly's Wife's behavior with the men on the ranch indicates the real possibility of childhood sexual victimization. Sharon's imagination keeps retrieving that possibility.

There are a few of points to cover. The first is prurience and inessential curiosity. Like a bad director who manipulates actors into sexual or dangerous emotional states, it would be easy for the dreamworker to do the same and worse. Both could cite artistic exploration and the perfect expressivity of the play as cover, but in fact they are motivated by prurience. Occasionally we all fall victim to unwholesome interest, so vigilance against this in yourself is essential when you dreamwork. It violates the trust between the actor and the dream-worker and could poison the well of the work. And it is unsavory because it is unnecessary.[9]

Some simple techniques to prevent against this are to ask the actor to experience something without revealing the details to you. You will see later that Robert asks Sharon to feel something in her body without telling him where is occurs. You can also limit the scope of the exploration by telling the actor that crossing into an extreme emotional state will be counterproductive, which Robert does when we continue Sharon's narrative.

There is another important issue that directs against probing too far. Sharon is incubating a memory that resides almost entirely within her own perspective. The playwright alludes to something offensive, but there is no substantiating evidence for it in the play, other than the behavior of Curly's Wife, which can be interpreted in several ways. Because Robert and Sharon are working on memory without suffi-cient documentation from the play, the memory of the character is colored almost exclusively by the actor. Exploring the act of abuse is contraindicated if only for that reason alone. You will see that Robert creates the potential for the abuse, the atmosphere of abuse, but does not forge into the act of abuse for which there is no documentation.

In other circumstances exploring sexual or emotionally explosive issues could be rightly on the agenda. They may be at the very heart of the character as represented by the text. If they are purely in the data of the play the dreamworker should proceed discretely but courageously. If you do not know the actor well, or if the actor is a

---

9. There are other, more psychologically intricate issues, like transference and countertransference, that could arise, but since this is not a book about psy-chology I'll mention them and move on.

reticent person, use directions like, "When you find where the feeling is located in the body observe it, but don't tell me." You will be surprised by how easy it is to work without knowing the precise details, and a few examples follow. If, however, the moment the actor wants to incubate stems from the text crying out for the exploration of sexual or otherwise eruptive material, and you have a solid, long-standing working relationship with the actor, you can work explicitly. The actor will know it is justified as long as you stand guard against your own prurience. The advantages here are twofold: it is at the heart of the actor's and the character's matter, and sensitive body parts are perceptive communicators.

Robert advises Sharon,

Sharon, you have to tell me how far to go. If you get too scared it is not useful. It doesn't add anything.

OK.

What kind of motel room is it?

It is ugly. None of my toys are there. It is not my room. I am just there with him sitting on the bed. He is talking about what it is going to be like.

Listen to him talk. What is his tone of voice like?

Trying to be soothing.

Does it calm you down?

Yes, it does.

What is it like?

I want to believe him.

As you feel how much you want to believe him, his voice is soothing.

Yeah.

And what does that do to you, this wanting to believe him and the soothing voice?

I am beginning to imagine with him.

What's that like?

That's great. Exciting, fun. I can't wait!

Locate that in your body.

My stomach.

Feel how exciting that is in your stomach.

Take a pause. Allow the sensation to develop. When you establish a node (an image complete with sensation, desire, metaphor) pause to allow it to develop and network. Robert pauses, then continues,

At any point does the mood change?

Robert's "At any point does the mood change?" is worth noting as a good, respectful leading question.

I don't know. I am scared. My concept of what happened is frightening. Is that where we are heading? I don't know if that is right.

What you imagine is what we are working with

OK. He is rubbing my back.

Does it feel good?

Yes, but it is also uncomfortable.

How do you begin to feel the discomfort?

In my stomach. It makes me tense

So in the same place where you felt the excitement before there is a shift?

Robert begins exploring the opposition in the in-between state.

Yes.

So can you feel how the shift in your stomach happens? Excitement to feeling sick in your stomach? Try to go just to the point where it is still excitement but just is starting to become sick in the stomach. What is it like again?

And once again, Sharon experiences the instability and warring tension of the moment between.

Struggle.

Like the one in the chest?

Yeah, it is.

Feel the struggle in the stomach.

With what happens next I would like you to not give me a graphic description. Just remember it, ok.

Yes.

Because you are working on unsubstantiated data when you work with memory alone, ask the actor to touch on the memory only long enough to identify where in the body she experiences sensation. Move away from memory entirely and work only with the physical. The embodied sensation contains the story fully without the tyranny of a play-by-play narrative. The body's organic glimpse encodes all that is necessary.

> As you remember it for yourself just let the memory in. Feel the location in your body where the memory is strongest. Don't tell me anything. Just allow the memory in. Keep your focus. Where in your body do you feel it strongest—or focus on the place in your body where you feel it strongest. Do you feel that?
>
> I am struggling with it a little bit.
>
> Just for a moment let the feeling in, just long enough to locate it.
>
> OK.
>
> That location in your body, feel into that location in your body. In your stomach feel the struggle of wanting to believe him and not believing him. You feel the struggle in your chest of the longing and the smell of the alcohol. In your head the feeling of wanting to curl under the covers.

The elements of Sharon's incubation image are networked in order to evoke the character's body influenced by her childhood abuse. Given the incubation event and the way that Sharon's imagined vision unfolded, Robert incubated oppositional transitional states instead of working sequentially, as he did with Jack. Selection of the imagery was based entirely on these transition. This is an important modality in dreamworking.

Because of the potentially upsetting nature of Sharon's incubation image, Robert suggested that she evoke it a half hour before bedtime, rather than while lying in bed. An emotional, wakeful actor decidedly would not produce dreams.

In Los Angeles, after Sharon and Michael Friedman played the scene the first time, we dreamworked Michael's character's body. In the break before they went back to act the scene for the second time, John Ruskin correctly suggested that Sharon had not extended a rich enough fantasy life to Curly's Wife. He led her through a perfectly clear substitution exercise in which Sharon replaced Curly's Wife's fantasy of the flashy Hollywood life she will have once she leaves the ranch with Sharon's personal fantasy.[10] When Sharon and Michael acted the scene again not much new emerged on the fantasy front.[11] Then Sharon told us her dreams.

> A couple of dreams were really fragmented, but one was clear and complete. I am on a boat going to Catalina. I ask where Avalon is. Someone says, "Through there." My mom was there—in life she has passed away. We went through a passageway, the entrance to a beautiful place. And my mom says, (I was there with a friend or maybe my niece), "Don't blink." And my friend says "Why is your mom saying not to blink?" And I say, "She doesn't want us to miss this." We went through and there was a sweet looking couple in a house on a hill. And I remember thinking, "Oh I'd like to be there." . . . And then I am with my niece and these boys make fun of her and she is really hurt. A little boy comes over to her and strokes her hair to comfort her.
>
> Another dream—A friend of mine is doing a scene with another girl and I was watching them. It was almost like she was doing a dance; she was snapping her head like this. She had a ski hat with a big puff on it. What they were doing was really good, and I felt jealous. Later, I am with her, and maybe her husband, and we pass a store. I say, "Oh, this is my favorite store." We go in and she tries on

---

10. An actor could walk through the landscape—and embody—her autobiographical fantasy in only slighly longer than it took to do this substitution without the embodiment. I think it would assure a more successful outcome. Just begin with, "What do you see?"

11. Michael Friedman's work was strong and able throughout.

a dress. I want it. She bought it. Then we are in a car. I have my baby with me and they want to smoke. They ask me if they can. I remember feeling offended by that.

In the last dream I see this girl who I haven't seen in a really long time and she has become a plus size model.

That last dream cracks Sharon—and the rest of us—up. Robert checks in with me for my opinion on which dreams to include. I suggest he add to his list the part of the dream when Sharon is jealous when her friend buys the dress she loves. Curly's Wife craves pretty things, both as a child and a woman. We all have our foibles, and Robert's is insensitivity to fashion and what it signifies; I knew he wouldn't value that part of the dream.

Robert enters with the plus size model because she made Sharon laugh. He moves quickly to the dress.

What about the dress bought by someone else? What was that like?
I felt jealous. We were in my favorite store.

Can you go to the moment when you first started to feel jealous?

It's a longing.

Where are you?

Outside the store.

Can you sense into the longing? How does it feel in your body?

It feels tired.

Sense into that tired longing. What is it like to be inside that tired longing in your body?

It's like I am really inside myself, but I want something—I want to be out.

Feel that. Where in your body do you feel that?

In my chest.

Focus on your chest and feel how you are really inside your body but want to be out.

Yeah.

Taking notes as they worked, I wondered why Robert hadn't anchored certain things into a visual and sensate loop. What was going on? Was his fashion disinterest affecting him? This was a mealy beginning. Robert moves to the next dream scene:

Can you describe where you are when you see the dancers?

Yes, I actually go into a dance class.

Can you see them move?

Yeah, they are far on the other side of the room. I want to go—I want to be there.

Feel how much you want to be there. Feel the location in your body how much you want to be there. What is it like to so much want to be there?

It is painful in my chest and heart.

Stay with it. OK, as you feel that can you look at the movement of the dancers?

It's very lyrical.

Can you feel that lyrical movement through your body? Keep feeling your heart and feel the lyrical movement go through your body. OK. Feel your body with the lyrical movement and the longing.

Reading back on the first and second movements of this dream-work, you see proof that selectivity is not a science. There is plenty of latitude. Had Robert worked the dress scene it would have likely yielded the identical physical theme as the dance scene—longing.

If, however, Robert had chosen to work the dress scene he would have first had to go to Sharon's perspective, then get her into the other woman's state, and finally into how the dress affects the woman.

To transit into "the other" you must first work away from the actor's ego perspective. If you try to make the jump without transitional steps, you will not be successful. You will stay stuck in the actor's perspective.

Robert favors taking the actor into "the other" through movement. When he saw the opportunity to enter into the dance, he went for it. His takes Sharon from her perspective → to watching the dance → to feeling the longing to "be there" → to identifying the location in her body where that longing is → *and finally* to feeling the lyrical movement through her body. He "fixes" the moment by wedding the longing in her heart with the lyrical movement. Robert describes Sharon's desire when she declares, "I want to be there," as the ore. He calls the moment she identifies with her desire, "It's very lyrical," the vein. He mined the desire and then had her transit into the identification.

When dreamworking, always be alert to an "entryway into another world." Here is a clear-cut example of embodying the entrance into the other world. It is a common enough dream theme, so it makes sense to look for it. Its reference back to *Of Mice and Men* is tenacious. As George waits for Lenny to enter the other world so he can "transport" him there, Curly's Wife anticipates her departure into the other (better) world that awaits her when she leaves the barn in the dark of night. And once again we enter through the other world via the mother. As she enters the passageway, Sharon's mother says, "Don't blink," in other words, "Keep your eyes open to the new world!" Robert then shifts the scene.

> Now, go to the moment when you are in the passageway.
>
> Yeah.
>
> Your mother says, "Don't blink." Feel it. As you feel it describe what you see.
>
> I see a beautiful island and trees. And the house.
>
> What is it like to have so much beauty in front of you?
>
> I want to be in it.
>
> Do you feel that desire to be in it?
>
> It feels good.

Responses like "good" and "bad" are generally useless. They are a wet blanket in comparison to her longing to "be in" the beauty in front of her. Robert returns to Sharon's evocative response and mirrors it back to her. Then he repeats it, asking her to let it affect her, and waits until it creates a networked response.

> Let the beauty work on you. Be affected by the beauty. Let it pervade your whole body. What is happening?
>
> I am breathing in the air. I want to be there with the ocean and the trees.
>
> Feel the air in your lungs.

The image entered fully into her body. She literally breathes the air of the other world. Robert can move on to another scene. In this next movement Robert asks Sharon to transit from her perspective to her niece's, and from there into the boy's perspective. These shifts are quick, but notice how rapidly Sharon complies with significant, embodied responses.

> Now, can you go to the moment when the little boy is stroking your niece's hair? Can you describe it?
>
> Yeah, she is little and she is hurt.
>
> Look at her and sense how hurt she is. Where in your body do you feel it?
>
> In my face.
>
> Feel your face. Can you feel her face being stroked?
>
> It's comforting.
>
> Feel in the hair how comforting it is. Can you still feel the face?
>
> No. Do you want me to?
>
> Yes, for a moment.
>
> OK.
>
> Now as you feel the hair being stroked in comforting ways, can you feel the hands that stroke? Are they stroking fast or slow?
>
> Slow.
>
> Is it a gentle stroke?
>
> Yes.
>
> Can you feel into the gentle stroke?
>
> Yes.
>
> Can you feel into his arms with the gentle stroke?

It's my hair now.

OK. Feel the rhythm of the stroke and the small hands. Do you feel the intention of the hands?

Yes.

Does he like it?

Yes.

Feel into his body and sense how much he likes it. What is it like in his body?

I feel like he feels sexual.

Sense how it is becoming sexual. What is it like in his body to become sexual? Where in his body can he feel that most?

In his lower body. It is powerful.

You don't have to talk about it, but focus on the part of the body that he feels it most.

OK.

Lenny has entered the landscape in precise imagery, a little boy stroking a hurt little girl's hair, duplicating the action of the scene between Lenny and Curly's Wife. Robert continues,

> Stay with your focus there, now feel the pain and the hurt of the little girl in the face. Now breathe the air of the beautiful place. Feel the lyrical movement go through your body. Now feel the intense longing in the heart. Now balance yourself in it. The air of the beauty in your lungs, the longing in your heart, the hurt in your face, the comfort in the hands, the power in the groin. Stay in that.

Robert composes Curly's Wife's dreamworked body of

- Contact with the environment: breathing the air of the beautiful place.

- Contact with the event: the intense longing in the heart (to be in the dance); the hurt in the face, the comfort in the hands that stroke.

- Contact with the other: the power in the groin.

Sharon and Michael play the scene. Everything changes. Sharon's voices drop down into her body; she is grounded in a real world. Curly's Wife enters the barn, walking the line between her dreadful present and her luscious future. Lenny's sight of the escape suitcase poses a much greater threat, and Curly' Wife is more menacing as a result. Her urgent fear of exposure lengthens the number of steps it takes Curly's Wife and Lenny to go on their relational journey. So when they finally arrive at a place of peace between them, they have traveled a distance in faceted steps. Lenny possesses glimmers of perception—he seems more human, however simple.[12] The two most striking elements are Curly's Wife's remembrances and her fantasies. The dream provides Sharon with the underlying actions of both actions. Her fond memory of her beloved father has a delusional quality that addresses Sharon's initial suspicion that Curly's Wife was

---

12. Michael Friedman dreamworked his body, and paralysis descended when he acted the scene immediately after. The next time he did the scene (after Sharon had dreamworked) he was as more plaint and lively, but only as much as Lenny could be. Michael suggested that time was the solution. "Maybe it's a grandiose analogy, but when the universe was created there was a huge explosion. It all came out of a big ball, and then it spread and went to different places. Things became less blocked. I feel it was the same with the dreamwork. The next time playing the scene it was not as overwhelming."

a victim of molestation. Instead of answering the question intellectually it provides the character with specific behaviors that suggest,
"This is the way a child who was sexually abused might have developed." We saw a woman comprised of dozens of twining cords, each
one a life experience. We'd rather not know about many of them. She
had no conscious knowledge of many of them. As Curly's Wife spoke
about her past successes that predict a glorious future, the audience
watched image after image pass through the character's body. Not a
word was uninformed.

In the discussion that followed Sharon reported finding the experience "intense." "A lot of imagery came in, some of it from my own
life. But even if they were from my life they had the same tone as the
dream images. I felt angrier entering. I felt like I was 'Getting Outta'
Here.' And when I talked about my old man being a drunk, I felt the
longing surge through me." Michael Friedman agreed that the work
"seemed to jar loose a lot of imagery for me. Not only images from the
dream, though some of those were there, too. It seemed like the dreamwork allowed me to find new things in both imagery and feeling."

At the least, the steps in the process had three outcomes. The
incubation preparation served as actor's research, walking the actors
down into the world of the play and into an intersection with their
characters. The embodied state produced by dreamworking the character's body was "digested, placed, and then available instantly." And
the dreamwork certainly served as excellent emotional preparation for
the scenes, although this was of least interest to me. These alone were
fine results with a group of actors we had not worked with before.
But of course the deepest consequence of the work was the
unearthing of a complex field of character. Out of the ten actors we
dreamworked in Los Angeles, nine discovered far more than emotion.
They dreamt their characters' dreams made out of the raw material
of their own lives in connection with the play. And by evoking the
embodied imagery for a few seconds and then letting go of it before

they walked onstage, they were possessed by the character. So much material presented itself that the actors could simply let it emerge, while still attending to the conscious choices every actor must make while on stage. They entered the scenes and found themselves quite suddenly feeling grounded in a world made much more vivid and etched by their characters' dreams. And most important to me, what emerged was not simple cause and effect. Layered effects materialized that truthfully sprang from a history I did not know but could recognize or intuit. And it all moved at the speed of perception.

CONCLUSION

In conclusion I offer a review of the variety of ways we've worked. Because we have experimented widely as we progressed, I outline a few different kinds of preparations. Every approach will work in some way. When I look back at the variety of these movements I can see how much we simply followed our noses, not knowing what we were doing. And even today, as I sit here writing about what we did and how we did it, a degree of postrationalizing is happily taking place. Indeed, we construed things from the process and its results that showed us what to intensify or otherwise alter. Some movements or manifestations felt immediately intrusive, or not "made of the same stuff," which became an excellent indicator of a wrong direction. Some things worked wonderfully and we intentionally went about building on them. But most often we worked impressionistically, and that remains true still. So while I have given you rules and some recipes, please go into the kitchen and cook up your own confection, as long as you remember to be respectful of the actor and to follow her lead.

On a brief note of what *not* to do, I remind you not to reintro-
duce material from the actor's life or from the play when preparing
the incubation image. When dreamworking the body don't bring
back information from the actor's life, the play, or the incubation
image. Keep all of the data in the same species.

There are two main modalities: working sequentially and working simultaneously. When you work sequentially you walk with the
actor through the landscape and impressionistically choose images to
embody. Let me give some examples of each modality and review any
unique movements that arise.

A Simple Sequential Incubation
Linda Tsang, from *The Seagull*

Linda was asked to sequentially re-experience the following sensations
that comprise the fully formed incubation image: (1) the chilly feeling
in her back—"like cold steel making contact with the bench;" (2) the
sight of the seagull's dead, "marble"-like, "beady" eye; and (3) the
sight of the "muddy" shoes. When she was able to move effortlessly
from one of these points to another, the process was complete.

These images draw from the actor's contact with the environment, the other, and the event she incubated.

A Lengthy Sequential Incubation, Transiting Freely into Characters and Objects
Jeremy Butler, from *The Illusion*
from Jeremy's journal entry

The scene that I incubated was seeing the tableau of my son stabbed
by the Prince. My first physical feeling was that everything below my
heart drops, all the blood, all the fluids in my body sink to the
ground. Then I focused on the blood coming from my son's wound. I
went into the Prince's body and the way he stands, and the tension

and relish in his body as he holds the knife. I go into the feeling of
his blood, how loud and hot it is. Then I move over into my son's
body as the knife is jabbed through his heart, which generates a feeling as if neoprene rubber covers his body and his head and face. He
wants to scream, but he can't.

Robert worked his way through the landscape and chose dynamic
images that evoked the horrid event being incubated: the moment
Pridamant witnesses his son's stabbing. But you can see that Robert
drew from Jeremy's sense of himself in the landscape, the event, and
the other.

Experiencing a Contrast Between Two Bodies
Manish Goyal's dream from *All's Well That Ends Well*

While exploring the dream Manish first inhabited the scornful look
on his ex-girlfriend's face. He then transited into Larry Hagman and
felt how Hagman looked upon him as an annoying boy, a "nonentity." Hagman, on the other hand, was brimming with sexual confidence and manly arrogance. Manish experienced Hagman's broad
shoulders and manly arrogance and how they were contrasted by a
physical imbalance he felt as he inhabited Hagman's body. He then
effortlessly re-experienced the marked contrast between Hagman's
broadness and the dream-Manish's delicacy.

Robert asks Manish to embody two contrasting body states and
then has him transit from one to the other and back. This movement
is like a painter laying one color next to another to create an apparent third thing by the contrast. If the actor can see what something
is not, then what it is comes into sharper relief. When you embody
the contrast between the self and the other, you must focus more
attention on the other because the self is so present. It was easy for
Manish to experience his own delicacy; he had to discover Hagman's
broadness and imbalance.

Working simultaneously is the other major modality or the dreamwork. Essentially is means that you hold embodied nodal points together. It breaks down into a few categories.

Simultaneously Holding Together Opposing or Contrasting Embodied States of the Same Character
Linda Tsang's Second Incubation from *The Seagull*

Linda experienced the sensations that followed from her/Nina being stifled at her father's home, and from the sensations resulting from her freedom on Sorin's estate across the lake. She then held both of these states together simultaneously. Embodying the tensions between these polar states and then *holding them together* created the seed that grew into Nina's pressing need to escape. In this instance we did not wait for a third state to emerge, but its presence was implied. Linda re-experienced each body-world, then held them together simultaneously as her incubation image.

Simultaneously Holding Together Opposing or Contrasting Embodied States and Waiting for a Third Body State to Emerge
Sharon Repass's Incubation in *Of Mice and Men*

As you want to hold him and you have the feeling in your chest, are you slowly starting to believe him?

I am trying to. It's hard. He smells like alcohol. I am trying, I think I can.

It's an effort. But I think I can do it.

Can you feel the effort?

Yes.

Focus on where the effort is.

Not breathing.

Not breathing and also feel the longing in the chest.

It's a real struggle.

Stay with that struggle. Feel it a moment longer so it is anchored.

The breathless struggle is the third body state that contains both opposing forces (the fear of the stinking father and the desire to believe him). Contrasting the two states, then hold the positive and negative poles together and the in-between state emerges. It was always present between the poles, but remained hidden until pressured to appear. Holding opposing states together intensifies the whole network.

Simultaneously Holding Together the Two Characters in a Scene to Create the Network Between Them
Alan Arkin's Incubation, *Virtual Reality*

As you listen now to the voice of the man who is reading, what is that voice relating to you?
It is an annoyance. Pushing.

Is there an intention of pushing in the voice?

No.

What is the mood of the voice?

It is trying to please, to do good, to be correct, but it is still pushing me.

Can you sense what it is like to try to please like that?

From the inside of it? I think so.

Keep on listening to it and feel what it is like from the inside of the
spoken voice. What kind of body comes from that sense of the spoken voice?

A lot of physical strength. Unaware of the extent of the strength.

Can you feel into that strong body that is unaware of the strength?

Yes. It feels good.

How is it different from the man on his knees?

It feels very integrated, very cohesive, of one piece. Younger, more
agile. There is a purity there.

Can you let yourself feel that purity throughout and see what happens to you?

There is a kind of innocence.

Where in your body can you feel that innocence?

My head.

Stay with the feeling in your head for a moment. Now go back to the
moment with the cloth when you feel your cold hands. Feel the lungs
that are filled with the smell of the cloth, invigorated. Can you feel
that?

When Robert asked, "How is it different?," he naturally evoked a
comparison between the two characters. By embodying both characters simultaneously (the man on his knees with the cloth tent-like
body and the strong, unaware younger man), Alan networked a new
response and a different body state emerged (the man with the innocence in the head). In *Virtual Reality* the two men literally create each
other's worlds, but isn't that systemic interaction a more nuanceed
fact in almost every play?

Simultaneously Holding All Images Together
as a Pressurized Whole
Anthony Arkin's dreamworked Body for *Virtual Reality*

Can you feel into [the Captain's] whole body—the gesturing arms, so much to do?

Yes. It feels wiry and strong.

Stay with that. . . . Now go to Anthony's melting. . . . Now go to the purging hair pulled through your thumb. Try to stay with these three body feelings: the melting, the purging, and the strong wiriness. What is it like to feel these three feelings?

Exhilarating.

Can you say what's happening to your body now?

It's an interesting combination of weak and strong, releasing and tension.

Stay with these three feelings. What is it like to stay in this body?

It feels healthy, but it also feels restless. I should do something with this body!

Holding images together as a pressurized whole is the most profound movement of the process. It initiates an intense networked response among all of its parts. The goal in Anthony Arkin's dreamwork was to create the character's body in response to the totality of the world of the play, which included the other character. If you envision each selected sensory image as possessing its own story, then holding all of them together creates a body comprised of all of those stories. Applying this movement as the final step in preparing an incubation image or in dreamworking the body catalyzes the deepest results. But remember—you may not always be after the deepest results. You may wish to solve a particular problem, address a specific issue. In that case you might still hold images together, but you would select only those images appropriate to your ends. Don't incorporate the whole world when all you are thinking about is a little corner.

The last issue to cover is that of working between dreams. As I wrote earlier, you will choose to work on dreams with obvious thematic relevance to the incubation image and the play. If you have a choice of several dreams, you'll choose scenes in which the imagery is richest, which may be those with the least connection to the actor's daily life. But when you are presented with two or three dreams that contain gorgeously imagined symbols and action, then feel free to select scenes from a few. The same genetic material, the incubation image, created them, and they will combine to effect the character's dreamworked body, which "bodies forth," as Shakespeare wrote,

> And as imagination bodies forth
> The forms of things unknown, the poet's pen
> Turns them into shapes, and gives to aery nothing
> A local habitation and a name.
>> *A Midsummer Night's Dream*, act 5, scene 1

And then there it is. The character's body appears before your eyes. She opens her eyes on a vivid world. The landscape is etched by her experiences. Memories arise unbidden in detailed images as she speaks. They shape her thoughts, and in turn her thoughts shape her words. When she casts her eyes on the other, together they play out events that only these two actors could originate. And the wide sea of imagination overlays their world. There is no threshold to cross because imagination is in everything, everywhere.

INDEX